JUST
GET
IT
DONE

Conquer Procrastination, Eliminate Distractions, Boost Your Focus, Take Massive Action Proactively and Get Difficult Things Done Faster

Som Bathla
www.sombathla.com

Your Free Gift Bundle

As a token of my thanks for taking out time to read my book, I would like to offer you a gift pack:

Click and Download your Free Gift Bundle Below

Claim Your Gift Bundle!

Three AMAZING BOOKS for FREE on:

1. Mind Hacking - in just 21 days!
2. Time Hacking- How to Cheat Time!
3. The Productivity Manifesto

Download Now

You can also download your gift at http://sombathla.com/freegiftbundle

More Books by Som Bathla

The Science of High Performance

Fast Track Your Success

The Mindful Mind

Conquer Your Fear Of Failure

The Mindset Makeover

Living Beyond Self Doubt

Focus Mastery

Just Get It Done

You may also visit my all books together at http://sombathla.com/amazon

Contents

CHAPTER I: INTRODUCTION

****

Oh, No, Not Again! A Cop stopped my car on my way to check my registration and other documents. Guess what happened? Anything wrong?

Yes, the "pollution under check" certificate of my car had expired two weeks ago, and I missed out getting it renewed, despite a reminder popping out a few days before the renewal date.

Sounds familiar! Take another one.

Another day, my boss asked that one urgent report to be finished by the end of the week. In my "expert" understanding, given the nature of work, it didn't seem to be that big a project. I thought to crank out a wonderful report in a day's time. So normally working on other things, I was waiting for Friday to start working on the report.

But, OMG, the work turned out to be a lot trickier, requiring me to do a lot more research on the topic, than I would have anticipated. I ended up producing the report in the last hours and that too shared with my seniors at the eleventh hour only. You must be again guessing what would have happened?

I ended up facing the music from bosses for delivering a less than perfect document and that too at the last hours.

Unless you are a genius or some superman, you might remember one or two such instances in your working life, right? So, what I was trying to convey through my real-life experience?

Firstly, I was honestly telling that procrastination is part and parcel of everyone's life and I suffer from that as well. Secondly and more importantly, I believe that most of you reading above will connect with above instances, as these keep happening frequently, in one way or the other in our day to day affairs.

Although, your examples might differ depending upon your personal circumstances and specific environment. But, the crux of the matter is that we all keep on lingering on certain things until the last possible moment. Isn't it?

Most of us don't file our tax returns even one month or even a few weeks in advance. We keep on waiting till the last date and then start rushing and making a phone call to our accountants. And this is despite being aware that in the last hours there is so much rush and panic around.

Why you can't get things done?

It is due to a chronic disease called "Procrastination," which has badly plagued most of our society in the modern-day world. The people end up suffering in all major areas of their life due to this evil; be it their family life, relationship, career, jobs, finances, etc. You might be wondering why one cannot do every small task immediately. There are always 36 other items on our agenda, which need to be addressed. Then, what is the role of prioritization in our waking hours?

After all, we only have only 24 hours in a day. Though, we keep on wishing that we had a few more hours in our lives, so we could enjoy the things which matter to us. Inspired by this very question, I had written my first book "The 30 Hour Day: ", solely to address this time management problem. (You can get further details about that at www.sombathla.com).

Anyways, we cannot increase our numbers of hours by clock time. It only requires some mindset shift and installation of a few smart habits to manage this limited resource prudently and effectively. But, let's get back to your question of the role of prioritization in our lives.

Firstly, thanks, that you have donned a critique's hat to test whether this book captures this important "human psychological issue" holistically. Even I would want to congratulate you for raising this, as this is a genuine expectation by anyone sincerely looking for a cure for this disease.

But let me assure you that this book addresses that aspect as well. It differentiates procrastination with prioritization. Rather, it goes one step further and touches the aspect of POP, i.e., Procrastination on Purpose. Stay tuned; you will get to know a lot more interesting and useful stuff here.

How Is This Book Structured?

Before we rush forward, I just want to give you a quick summary of what you should expect from this book. Though the table of contents beacons toward the topics, I want to have a brief conversation with you to explain as to how you should approach this book. The book goes in a sequential manner, i.e., explain the disease, its symptoms, the differentiators with other similar appearing stuff, the diagnosis or analysis, the key contributors to that disease. And finally, with all this awareness, once you are prepared, it shows you the strategies to treat this with acquired confidence.

But why I have not simply shown the strategies immediately in front of you and filled up so many pages before that? There is a genuine reason behind it. It is because:

"80% of Success is psychology, and 20 % is mechanics – Tony Robbins"

While most of us intellectually know the above, but honestly, I have had personally experienced this a number of times in my life. In other words, once you are psychologically prepared for anything, you stick to the strategies and tactics.

Okay, the book is structured as below:

- It **defines procrastination** with the help of practical illustrations.

- It <u>distinguishes</u> procrastination (a disadvantage) with **prioritization and Procrastination on Purpose (POP)** (a Virtue).

- It narrates **what kind of code procrastinators use** for staying with and justifying their instinct of procrastination.

- One full chapter captures the **OS (operating system) of the minds of a procrastinator (mindset) and compares with a non- procrastinator's mindset**. It gives you insights and explains the key difference in the mentality of both these persons.

- The book goes on further to explain numerous reasons, which people sell to themselves to justify their act of procrastination (and on the face of it, they seem very honest, innocent and genuine, but let me tell you, underneath it is all mental bullsh*t (BS) only- we will cover that in detail). One full-blown chapter goes on to elaborate as to **why do people procrastinate** in most of their affairs despite being aware that it has neither served in the past and nor it is not going to serve them in the long run?

- Lastly, the meatiest and lengthiest portion of this book, **27 effective and proven strategies implemented by the**

productivity super-stars to beat procrastination and rock their performance to the next best level. You will learn how to start implementing these techniques in your days to boost up your results instantly.

I am sure you must be feeling excited (as I am getting while writing this), to jump directly into the contents. But one last doubt you might have, if you have not seen my other work already (see at www.sombathla.com). Let us spend a minute on that as well. What's that doubt?

Why Should You listen to me?

So, who am I to talk about this monstrous topic, with a promise to eradicate this "procrastination" menace from your life? Let me put it a very straightforward way.

No, I am not any specialist or expert in this field. I am a next-door guy who simply has tried to understand the life principles from reading multi-dozen books on productivity, human psychology, behavior, human potential, etc. Further, I have taken further steps and tested many of the principles as narrated in those books. And based on my experience, I can vouch that these principles definitely work if one is committed to putting some actions around them.

So, to put it shortly, I have personally explored, learned and implemented these principles and these have worked for me including writing this book and my previous books (more on that later). I have worked in the corporate world for more than a decade and a half out of my presence on this planet for around four decades now. In all this time, I came across various situations, and I tried my level best to handle these situations through my learning of these principles. I succeeded a lot of times, but failed miserably at other times, due to my lack of depth in understanding the principles. I think that all this makes me eligible to share my thoughts with my readers. The key challenge always is to put such an important subject cohesively so it can benefit the reader and help him or her lead their life better.

Secondly, I believe that when you plan to spread a message to the world in any manner (like this book here) it builds a moral pressure upon you to practice what you preach. I believe myself to be a life-long student and explorer and have done my best to follow most of the practices covered in this book (succeeded, as well as failed at times, but experiments are still on). But as you know, life is a journey and there is always room for improvement.

"Success is a journey, not a destination. The doing is often more important than the outcome"~ Arthur Ashe

So, I believe that writing this book will help me to be more responsible and accountable for living the principles stated herein. It will be a tool for me for self-observation and continuous improvement (I am selfish here ☺). The experience and drive to learn the new things in life make me eligible for writing and publishing this book.

Okay, let's get started now.

****

CHAPTER 2: PROCRASTINATION- DREAM KILLER (A GOOD FRIEND TOO)

****

"A man who procrastinates in his choosing will inevitably have his choice made for him by circumstance"~ Hunter S. Thompson.

Let's look at few statements below:

- I will do it a bit later.
- Some other urgent things have popped up, so I will start working on this report tomorrow.
- I am feeling very low on energy, so tomorrow morning is the best time to start it.
- It is already so late today, so it would be better to start this task with a fresh mind in a day or two.

- Too much has changed since the start of this week, so better I defer the earlier scheduled activities later.

Sounds familiar? Okay, let's hear a few more:

- Let me binge over another few episodes on Netflix and then start this work.
- Better I enjoy a few drinks with my friends this evening and then start working on the report tomorrow.
- These stinker emails from one of the clients have already spoiled my mood for the day and I can't focus on that important project now in this state of mind.
- I don't feel like doing it or I don't want to do it today. And it can be done tomorrow.

This is another set of statements (I will tell you in a bit why I put these two differently). The above are two different sets of statements, which we generally tell ourselves at times and also keep on hearing from people in our surroundings. But why do we react to the situations this way?

Okay, firstly, let's admit that our days are getting full of endless tasks, priorities popping up every now and then, thanks to the pace at which the information technology is emerging. The means of communication have become so widespread that anyone can steal your attention at any moment -- you know, email notifications, WhatsApp messages, facebook, twitter beeps and 20 other networks creating noise or vibrations in your head.

Unfortunately, the number of hours per day will remain only twenty-four and are not going to increase any more as compared to mounting workloads in front of us. So, what happens at the end of the day? A natural reaction i.e., a feeling of being overwhelmed! We tend to lose control over our work schedules. And procrastination seems to be the only response to these seemingly overwhelming scenarios. But apart from a mounting number of tasks, there are some natural human psychological reasons.

I have stated two different sets of statements above. Go back above and read them again.

What is the difference?

While the former set of statements indicates that a person is procrastinating the work because the amount of work is piling up and up and there is a feeling of being overwhelmed, which is then taking the form of procrastination. But the other set of statements is because of the human psychology and natural tendencies, due to which a person chooses to defer the urgent activity in order to give him or her a dose of instant gratification in some or the other form.

So, the procrastination confronts our lives in different forms and shapes (more on that in the next chapter). At some times, you may call it the prioritization of the work or at other times, you would say that you purposefully chose to procrastinate any particular task.

You might get confused sometimes, as there is so much hype around beating procrastination. There are numerous books available on the subject, which explain quick tools and tactics to beat the procrastination monster.

But hang on...Let's not kill the wrong bird in a hurry. Before you go on further to learn how to kill procrastination, you need to clearly understand what kind of delay or deferment could be considered as procrastination. As I have insisted in the previous chapter, we need to be sure that we understood the problem thoroughly before we even think about finding a solution for the same.

We will now go deeper into understanding the definition and the symptoms of procrastination. Also, to make it ultra-clear, we will see the explicit differentiation of procrastination as compared to prioritization and procrastinate purposefully. So, let's keep moving.

What is Procrastination?

Looking at a few quotes below on procrastination would help us to see how our educated predecessors have understood and explained procrastination differently.

> *"Nothing is so fatiguing as the eternal hanging on of an uncompleted task"* ~ *William James*
>
> *"If you want to make an easy seem job mighty hard, just keep putting off doing it"* ~ *Olin Miller*
>
> *"Procrastination is the thief of time"* ~ *Edward Young.*
>
> *"Procrastination usually results in sorrowful regret. Today's duties put off until tomorrow give us a double burden to bear; the best way is to do them in their proper time"* ~ *Ida Scott Taylor.*

We all know that the procrastination being talked about in the above quotes is a vice, not a virtue.

The Dictionary's meaning of procrastination is "the action of delaying and postponing something". Simply put, procrastination means deferring certain actions to be taken at a given point in time to a future date, despite knowing the negative consequence of not doing them in time, without any justifiable reason for such deferment.

For example, we all know that exercise is good and much needed for better health and fitness. We know that it is very necessary for better physical and mental stamina. But except for a few determined ones, who choose to put on their sports gear and move out, most of us keep pushing the snooze button on the alarm, until such time, it becomes the utmost necessity to get out of the bed. What urgency has come up to defer the important activity towards health?

Nothing! It is only procrastination.

Another example; you have to submit a report to your boss or your client by the end of the day today, which you know is time-bound. You already know that if not delivered in time, it is going to affect your credentials and reputation in your office or with the client.

Still, you chose to waste your time in gossiping around or getting distracted by other miniatures activities or getting stung with social media distraction bugs. You clearly know that there is no other priority of the work except that important report to be delivered by today at the end of the day, but still, you delay in starting your work until the eleventh hour. What is all this?

Simple, procrastination! What else?

Okay, now let's talk about some distinctions of Procrastination!

Distinction #1: Prioritization

Let's be clear here. It is not that every decision of ours to delay or postpone the things can be notoriously termed as procrastination. Those readers, who have spent enough time working for living through jobs or on their own, can easily cite the examples, when you had no choice but to postpone the work. Because something more important has come up! So important that the previous work, which was thoroughly significant, gets easily overshadowed by this new assignment.

So, what do you do?

While delay or deferment of both the works is costing you, there is a huge degree of difference. The difference could be in the amount of monetary loss or loss of a fatter business opportunity or losing your job or your most important client. Whatever the reason is, suddenly, this new item sits as item no. 1 on your To-Do-List.

Now the only rational choice in front of you is to: Prioritize or say re-prioritize. And the good news is that it is not procrastination of the earlier important work. In such cases, it is rather a prudent decision to focus on more significant activities. It is totally unwise to term this kind of deferment as procrastination. After all, life is all about making the right choices. The wiser choices you make, the better your life is.

You have not delayed the previous work, without any illogical reasons or rationale, rather you have intentionally chosen to defer it to safeguard your situation or optimize your ROTI (return on time invested). This is prioritization.

"Good things happen when you set your priorities straight" ~Scott Caan

Differences between Procrastination vs. Prioritization

Every delay, deferment or postponement cannot be called procrastination and we should not unnecessarily get into a guilt trap for such important deferments. Let's be very specific and clear about what procrastination is and what prioritization is.

Procrastination means that one is required to perform certain activities in a given timeline, but due to various reasons like distractions from social media, our network or due to our craving for indulging in something else, one chooses to delay the performance of such activities. In other words, if one chooses to delay the performance of some action solely because of factors which were under one's total control, merely to enjoy the feeling of instant gratification at the cost of key action, then it is definitely an act of procrastination. Certain examples will clarify this.

If you were supposed to work on your office report or to draft a presentation for clients, or write a blog article or finish a chapter for your next book (choose any action important to you), but while starting that or in the middle of that, you get certain mixed feelings of below nature:

- I think I should binge-watch some episode of Netflix before I get going on this project.
- Maybe it is a good idea to start this tomorrow morning, as it is already half the day gone.
- Shouldn't we go out to watch the latest movie this week, instead of working on that damned work project? After all, life is too short and we should enjoy it fully.
- And the list goes on and on.

For example, I am writing a chapter in this book, but suddenly thoughts are popping about making some tweaks on my website or checking my social media if there is any update. Now I have to make a rational choice as to where do I re-focus my attention amongst the different voices running in my head. On the surface, it looks like things are not in my control, but believe me; it is quite straightforward. You have either of the two choices:

- Either you choose to enjoy the instant gratification from the activities appearing as distractions to your important work, which you will do solely at the cost of your key project.

- Or else you make your instant gratification monkey silent by making a conscious choice and focus on your key project, which will give you the long-term rewards in the form of a completed office project, accolades from the client, publishing of your next blog post or completion of your first or next book.

Thankfully, I have chosen to silent the instant gratification monkey and have focused on working on this book, which has made it possible for this book to reach into the hands of my esteemed readers.

Now let's take another example of what can be termed as "prioritization."

It is already Thursday, and you are working on preparing for your Monday morning meeting with your customer/client, which has the potential of retaining that key client by way of renewal of the annual contract. Suddenly, you get a phone call from one of your reputed and wealthiest clients referring to a conference happening this Sunday, where there is a possibility of meeting dozens of other clients and seems there is a huge business potential. You clearly understand the kind of preparation needed to explain your product or services to the new set of people.

Now there is a dilemma.

On the one hand, you have an existing client, whom you are already serving and seeking renewal of the contract. But on the other hand, there is a potential of creating a funnel of a new set of clients or customers, which will provide financial rewards for the months and years to come. So, what would you do now?

Yes, you will try to postpone the existing clients' meeting for a few days, so that you can better prepare after you have attended that important conference. However, if somehow the client doesn't agree to change the schedule, then you will do better to postpone the preparation for the meeting with this client, until after the conference with prospective clients is over. In this case, you will choose to be comparatively lesser prepared for the existing client meeting, by changing your priorities. But you did your cost-benefit analysis already and were aware that this postponement is primarily to generate the further multiple revenue generation opportunities.

It is not procrastination; rather this is prioritization of your activities and is very much warranted in such scenarios.

Distinction #2: Procrastinate on Purpose- A Good Friend

The title of the book speaks of killing procrastination, and we are talking about purposely procrastinating. Surprising, isn't it?

But let's have a deep dive into this subject. Remember, we talked about POP in the previous chapter! What is this POP?

Procrastinate on Purpose (POP) is rather a very positive side of procrastination. This term was used in his best-seller book **"Procrastinate on Purpose"** by author Rory Vaden. In his book, Rory has gone one step further and has defined POP as a measure of creating or multiplying your time. He has categorically made an intriguing distinction between prioritization and POP.

He states that in prioritization, you don't create any further time for you. Rather you defer one activity now standing at #1 to item no #9, but you don't create any further time because you have to do that activity later on, once you have ticked your earlier eight items on your list. So, prioritization is a just reshuffling of activities in a different sequence and fitting them into your schedule.

He goes on to explain that in the POP concept, the Individual looks at the activity and uses the **"Focus Funnel"** methodology. In this focus funnel, any activity is divided into two major baskets, namely (1) Priority Dilution; and (2) Priority Concentration.

Let's understand this further (there is diagram later in this section to explain it better)

1. Priority Dilution

In this approach, look at the upper part of the Focus Funnel; you have three choices, sequentially as below:

1. You see if the activity can be totally eliminated from your schedule.
2. If not, you have to check if you can automate the activity, i.e., through some systems or tools, whereby it

happens with your least or no involvement at all.

3. If systems or tools can't serve the purposes, then you examine whether the activity can be delegated further.

Please note that in this approach you tried your best to dilute the priority level of the activity to the best level possible. This way, the effort was to save the time, which could be utilized for more value generation activities.

Now, next comes another basket, only after you have exhausted the first basket.

2.Priority Concentration

Once you determine that the activity does not fit into any choice of the Priority Dilution category, i.e., it is not possible to either eliminate, automate or delegate the activity, then you know that you have to devote your concentration towards the execution of that activity. But you don't stop here.

You again see whether this activity requires to be attended to immediately or if you can still allocate a specific time for this activity in the future or defer it for the future. The parameter for deciding whether to be done in the future or today is by measuring it through the metric of "significance." Here you check whether the action to be done is significant enough, i.e., does it create time for you in the future if you spend time on it today (see examples to understand this better)?

If you have exhausted the final opportunity and ascertained that the activity could not be further deferred to a future date (without any adverse ramifications), ONLY then you conclude that now you have to devote your time and concentration on this activity. The below diagram explains the concept succinctly:

(Image courtesy: "Procrastinate on Purpose" Book by Rory Vaden)

Let's try to understand above by way of an example:

You have a conference out of town to attend 6 months from today. You may want to book the ticket now and tick your box and be happy that you have not done procrastination in this activity. You may also think that you have saved money by getting cheaper tickets.

However, someone else could have taken a different option here. Since the meeting is six months down the line and even if I buy tickets three months from now, still it is three months in advance, so I can plan to buy the tickets three months down the line (without much difference in cost saving). What do I get by postponing this?

- I may think of and plan on meeting some of my friends in that town, so I could freeze my itinerary flexibility after talking to a few people.
- I might consider exploring the town with my family and combine this as a family trip, after doing some research on the tourism option.
- I may also explore any other business opportunity in that town and would want to stay longer.

Now the second option is quite beneficial, as it keeps open a much better flexibility to plan your trip without costing you further. However, if you chose the option one, merely to appear as a productivity ninja and get a false sense of accomplishment that you crossed one more item out of your list; it kills the flexibility of your travel option. Now, after booking the tickets, so much in advance, if you chose to change the tickets or extend the dates, etc. it will cost you much more.

So, this is a great example of POP. You noticed that all the possible choices in the Focus Funnel have the end of the objective of creating time for you, rather than merely reshuffling the priorities up and down in your to-do-list, as is done in the prioritization approach.

Hopefully, the concept of procrastination vis-a-vis other similar sounding phenomena, i.e., prioritization or procrastination on purpose is clear now. Now with that, we will ride this journey further to understand the psychology behind the procrastinator's mindset with key reasons and then how to tame the procrastination monster as well. Let's keep going. We have lots of interesting stuff to cover yet.

****

CHAPTER 3:
PROCRASTINATORS' CODE-
AN ESCAPE ROUTE

****

"Do you know what happens when you give a procrastinator a good idea? Nothing!"~ Donald Gardner

Try to remember or recall some instances from your memories. The chances are that you might have consciously or unconsciously noticed some common patterns while interacting with people in your surrounding environment. Because, whenever you or any other people in your working atmosphere tend to delay or defer certain things, there are some often repeated stances for such delay or postponement.

You would notice that anyone who is trapped in the procrastination habit (to whatever extent), would be found expressing a certain standard set of language to offer a proper justification for his or her procrastination. The below statements will help you to somehow relate to the inner circus going on in the mind of a procrastinator.

- I must be perfect in whatever I deliver, without even a punctuation mark mistake.
- If it is not done right, then it should not be done at all.
- It is safer to do nothing than to take a risk and get challenged.
- What will people think about me, if I don't appear to be perfect?
- It is better to wait until you are totally sure that there will be a positive outcome.
- If I perform well this time, I always have to deliver very well.
- What is the downside, if I do it a bit later or don't do it at all?
- I should not be in a hurry and take my full time.
- I can only work once I am inspired to, and I will wait for inspiration to arrive.

I call this language "**Procrastinator's Code**." No offense to any specific person, but only for the sake of easy reference, we will use the term Procrastinator for anyone and everyone suffering from procrastination (to any degree whatsoever). To be upfront, most of us, in some manner or to some extent, struggle with the menace of procrastination in our day to day affairs. I have shown a few examples already.

However, if none of the above statements apply to you, then you probably do not require this book. Still, you may choose to read this to validate your concepts about how to cure this procrastination disease.

So, coming back to Procrastinator's Code! Anyone can imagine that with this kind of thought process, how one can even think of moving one step further. Such mindsets promote the being standstill, indecisive and the better wait and watch approach in life. Because:

"What we think, we become"~ Buddha

And the irony is that the procrastinators put smoke screens so innocently over their minds that they don't feel any guilt or gloomy feeling for not taking action. They are able to get one or the other excuse to defer taking action on the activities listed on their To-do-list. And in that moment of deferring the activities for the future, it feels so real to them that postponing of such activity was the only right thing to do.

Just to give you another honest example, while I am writing this particular section of the book. The thoughts have just come to check the reviews of the latest movie released a few days ago that I plan to watch this weekend. Also, another sensation is prompting me to check my Facebook to see whether I still got 100+ likes on my yesterday evening's post of amazing family dinner clicks with friends. And... You see, I am writing a book on providing the solutions to the Procrastination problem, Huh! One can easily imagine the severity of this evil monster.

Strangely, when we defer our key activities, we act so foolishly despite being aware that completing our key activities is much more important to stick to, rather than digressing to other mundane activities or distractions, which in fact, can be deferred until we complete our main task.

Surprisingly, when things are so obvious, then why do most of the people still get bogged down and don't take any action on it?

Before we address that, let's try to understand the process or mechanism to overcome any problem. In my view, for resolving any kind of problem out there, the straightforward approach is always a four-stage process in order of sequence:

1. **Stage 1**: First and foremost, identify what exactly is the problem or concern.
2. **Stage 2**: Find out the reasons for such problem- ascertain all reasons- whether within our control or not.
3. **Stage 3**: Listing the alternative solutions to the problem, by utilizing our own life experience or by taking advice from others, who might have faced such problem.

4. **Stage 4**: Taking action or implementing the best possible alternative.

The key point to note here is that most people get stuck at the second stage only. They identify that there is some problem and allocate certain reasons as to why this problem is there. But they stop there only, putting the blame on the economy, their life circumstances, government, relationships, financial situation, etc., in a nutshell, they find enough reasons to choose not to move any further.

Rather, they are so plagued by the negative belief system that they even don't go a step further to check if there is any solution to that problem. Just on this related note, I wanted to tell you that in my previous book "**The 30 Hour Day**", I have written a complete chapter on the types of negative mindsets which kill our productivity and how to replace them. People use procrastinator's code generally at the second stage only. With the mindset fixed and infected by the procrastinator's code, people don't take any action to move further.

The problem is much graver, because, our minds are capable of deferring even such activities, which have clear-cut timelines to meet (and we know the adverse ramification of not doing those activities). So, with this procrastinating mindset, how would you be able to even consider working towards your dreams or ambitions for which there are no timelines fixed by us.

This point is very important, so let me emphasize this by putting it in different words. If you choose not to meet the timelines of any activity, which is imposed by external circumstances, then how will you ever be able to even start working on to achieve your dreams or ambitions? Because here no one from the outside will come and tell you to achieve that dream in 3 months or 3 years timelines. Rather it is you who has to craft a life by putting timelines and actions to catch your dream.

Tim Urban in his very famous TED talk (more than 13 Million views at the time of this writing) has explained the seriousness of this problem. You can watch the video at the link http://sombathla.com/timurban-tedtalk

He states that whenever there are external timelines given to any procrastinator, and the deadlines are approaching nearer, there appears a "panic monster." This panic monster threatens the deadly 'instant gratification monkey' sitting in the procrastinator's head to immediately work on the particular assignment. So that way, a procrastinator gets to work and deliver on that activity.

Then comes the interesting part! He goes on further to highlight the gravity of the situation by explaining that unfortunately, there is no such timelines and schedule given to achieve your dreams, so that means that if you are in the habit of procrastinating anything and everything, then you won't be even able to consider starting your first step towards your dreams. <u>Simple Reason, you don't take a step until the panic monster threatens you, which won't ever come to scream at you to work towards your dream</u>.

The procrastinator is always at the risk of not ever living his or her dream life, thanks to the procrastinator code so boldly tattooed in his mind.

"Procrastination is one of the most common and deadliest of diseases, and its toll on success and happiness is heavy" ~ *Wayne Gretzky*

Okay, now, let's get to understand one level further -- how the mindset of a procrastinator works on an entirely different approach as compared to a non-procrastinator.

****

CHAPTER 4: 5 BUGS IN PROCRASTINATOR'S MINDSET

****

If you have seen my earlier books (if not, you may check them out at www.sombathla.com), you will notice that I am a strong proponent of understanding the role and functioning of mindset in each area of life. Therefore, you will find a chapter on the mindset in each of my books.

It is because, once we understand the role of mindset about any problem, it does not take long to implement any change required to resolve the problem. Sometimes, it is just a quick shift in the brain neuropathways, and you see the world entirely with a different, new and positive perspective. You don't remain the same as you were before without having this updated understanding of how the mind functions.

In this chapter, you will have a chance to peep inside the mindset of a procrastinator. In other words, you will be able to make out why a procrastinator thinks the way he or she thinks. To make the understanding clearer and to enable the necessary mindset shift, this chapter explicitly lists the distinctions between the mindsets of a procrastinator and a non-procrastinator. Once you understand the *Modus Operandi* (mode of operation) of how your mindset works, you will often give yourself a chuckle when the mind starts to play tricks with you.

It is very difficult to independently examine your own mindset because it is like looking into our own eyes with our eyes. But once you get disengaged with your own mind, then you claim your gift of an unbiased overview of your thinking. And believe me; it is worth putting efforts to gain that understanding.

So, come on. Let's put our magnifying glasses on and start to peep inside the mindset of a procrastinator. Alongside that we will differentiate the same with the mindset of a non-procrastinator, to make the distinction quite visible.

1: Reactive Mindset (vs. Proactive Mindset)

The procrastinator has a reactive mindset for any activity or situation. He or she doesn't believe in preparing for the events much before; rather he chooses to react to the situation when it arrives. So, you can say that instead of making the necessary preparation for an important event, a procrastinator mindset believes that he will handle the situation when it comes close to him or her.

Only the panic monster (remember this friend, we talked in previous chapters!) makes a procrastinator tremble at the last minutes and forces him to take required action and that only at the very last stage. Until the panic monster knocks on the door, the procrastinator keeps on deferring the work as long as he can. On the other hand, a non-procrastinator is motivated and takes a proactive approach to every situation. He or she believes in preparing in advance and handling the work within time.

A procrastinator primarily thinks that things can be deferred and still he or she can very well be able to manage the situation even at the later stages. Why does this happen?

Due to Miscalculation! Yes, a procrastinator does not properly calculate the number of steps or outside dependencies involved in any situation. He does not put the effort into making a reverse calculation of the action steps required to be completed by the given timelines starting from today. Therefore, he or she is unable to understand the clear action steps or and external dependencies to be addressed to meet the deadlines.

On a false presumption, he thinks that he or she will be able to complete the work when it is very close. This person can be compared with a sitting pigeon, which has closed its eyes and thinks that there is no cat and he is safe, just because he is not able to see the cat. As soon as the deadline approaches near and the tasks and the outside dependencies start looming large, then panic monster shows its horror face to a procrastinator. Then there is no choice except to react.

Now your boss or your client or customer starts questing about the deliverable and you are really feeling overwhelmed merely by the sight of the heap of tasks on your desk.

So, what is the solution?
To transform his reactive approach to a proactive approach and get rid of the procrastination beast, one has to immediately start making calculations (if not starting the work itself), to get an idea of the steps to be taken and external dependencies to be addressed to complete the work in a given timeline.

2: Instant Gratification Mindset (vs. Long-Term Perspective Mindset)

The Procrastinator has a mindset to focus, and he or she easily gets swayed away towards instant gratification. In other words, whatever thing or activity gives an immediate pleasure or enjoyment, he or she moves towards that. While doing so, he or she does not pay any attention to the long-term implication of such choice.

For example, if there is a choice between watching a movie on Netflix, sitting on a couch with full-size pizza and coke vs. going to the gym, what choice a procrastinator will make?

With his instant gratification mindset, whichever option gives an instant pleasure will be the first choice. So obviously, in the given case, a procrastinator will prefer enjoying a movie with tons of junk food instead of working out at the gym. Because going to the gym is quite a lot of activity for him or her. One has to get up, put on the sports gear, get out of the comfort of home and then hit the instruments at the gym.
And what is the instant reward for going to the gym?

Nothing (Rather there is instant pain or discomfort)! However, there is the long-term benefit of maintaining a fit body, full of vitality and energy during the whole day and you may even have an opportunity of boasting of your six-pack abs (for men) or get praise for your slim and toned body (for women) if you continue longer.

You choose any real-life circumstance; a procrastinator mindset will always choose the option which is a quick reward and which does not require putting any efforts. Let's look at few of these examples to understand this instant gratification mindset clearly:

- Between going out to watch a movie vs. reading your professional subject book or any other personal growth material, the choice will be the former.
- Between binging on the junk food and drinks vs. following a healthy diet full of fresh fruits and vegetable, the choice will be former.
- Boarding up in the building by an elevator vs. going by stairs (even if it is just 1 or 2 floors), again the former will be the choice.

The procrastinator is convinced that he will take only that action that gives him or her an instant level of gratification or comfort. The 'long-term result' things are not the cup of tea for the procrastinator.

So how this can be corrected?

There is a way.

The activities, which have long-term results need to be somehow, presented before the procrastinator in such a way that he or she sees some instant benefit in doing that as well. For example:

- The option of going to the gym with your girlfriend seems to be giving an instant reward ☺+ longer term benefit.
- The option of watching Netflix, but looking at some entertaining and motivation movie will serve the dual purpose, i.e., entertainment plus personal development, rather than watch sex and crime thrillers.
- Similarly making your healthy food flavored and presented stylishly, may attract you more than eating boiled vegetables or soups.

So here you are able to use the weakness of procrastinator's mindset and make this as its strength. How?

Precisely by combining some elements of instant gratification in the long term beneficial project. You can see, the procrastinator's mindset will gradually start shifting little bit in very short period (you will get more on this in the strategies chapter).

3: Overwhelming Mindset (Vs. Clean Table Mindset)

The procrastinator mindset kicks you in the butt only when things become too overwhelming. So, whatever the situation is and howsoever the anxiety and stress levels are, the procrastinator now has to do it. On the other hand, a non-procrastinator believes in the clean table.

I have a close relative, whom I have seen occasionally working even beyond office hours. Upon questioning why he works at home, if there is no deadline for today and these things can be delivered tomorrow, his response was eye-opening and very convincing. He stated, *"I want my table to be totally clean when I reach the office the next day. It helps me have a good night's sleep and then a great morning next day till I reach my office to conquer the work of the next day."*

So, while a procrastinator is unable to work unless he or she is pushed against the wall, a non-procrastinator intentionally chooses to clear up his desk, even if he or she has to occasionally put in extra hours to buy that peace of mind.

So, how to mold the overwhelming mindset?

The only carrot that you can dangle before a procrastinator is to convince him that to get an instant reward of some peace of mind and a stress-free day tomorrow, things need to be handled today, before they get out of your control.

But this advice comes with a caveat that this should not become a day to day feature of your life, else you will get into another extreme category known as a workaholic (someone rightly stated that excess of anything is bad, even if that thing is good).

4: It's Easy-will do it later Mindset (vs. Do it Now Mindset)

The procrastinator's general approach is that things should be easy and he or she should be able to handle it later, even if he works at the last moment. Whereas, the non- procrastinator's approach is that even if the work is super-easy, why defer it to a later moment. You never know what new thing may come up in the future to significantly eat up your time and result in non-completion or delay in delivering the so-called easy project.

While the procrastinator underestimates the quantum of work involved (as explained in one of the previous points) in any particular project, the additional uncertainty of the future, with further items getting queued on the desk, plays a double whammy for the procrastinator.

This approach can only be changed by developing the discipline muscle and consistent practice of not delaying the work until the last stage. It will take time and effort, but it's worth putting in the effort (more on that later in the "How to" chapter).

5: Confused or Fearful Mindset (vs. Faithful about Future Mindset)

Also, it is a general tendency of the procrastinator to get confused about whether or not the action being taken is the right one, or if it needs to be changed. He (or she) keeps on doubting the action despite having started on the project. The procrastinator gets confused that whether the approach taken is the right one or if it needs to be modified in some way.

Whereas, the non-procrastinator works on faith, and has a stronger belief that the things will work out, and stays put in the game. The non-procrastinator's life mantra is:

"Everything is figureoutable" – Marie Forleo

This very belief system that things will work out in the future if one keeps going is one of the key factors in motivating a non-procrastinator to keep moving despite there being clouds of doubts overshadowing the clarity of the thinking process.

So, one needs to develop a strong faith in taking actions and believing that things will work out in the way which is most beneficial for oneself.

****

CHAPTER 5: 11 REASONS WHY PEOPLE PROCRASTINATE

****

"Procrastination is the art of keeping up with yesterday"~ Don Morquis

Good to see you here so far, with me. By now, you would have understood or would have validated your own earlier understanding that procrastination is a matter of serious concern. And like any other problem, before you move further to find a solution to the problem, you would want to understand the root cause of the problem. It is like a diagnosis of any disease in our body.

The first thing we want to understand from our physician or doctor is the precise reason or cause of such illness or disease. Assume your doctor is not forthcoming about telling you the exact reason and simply writes a prescription for medicines. How would you feel?

Of course, you would start doubting the doctor's advice and even doubting the effectiveness of the prescribed medicines as well. So, psychologically you start feeling that maybe this medicine will not work or this doctor is unable to diagnose the problem accurately. Moreover, if you are unaware of the exact reason of your illness, you would not be sure of what went wrong and what kind of precautions you need to take going forward to avoid such disease or illness in the future. In all probability, you would not prefer to visit that doctor again.

Therefore, applying the same principles here, you would want to be sure about what could be the reason for your procrastination disease. It is worth highlighting here that we all are crafted differently. We all had different life circumstances, a very different upbringing, different social networks, and different work environments. So, there cannot be one set of answers to the procrastination problem which each of us faces in our everyday lives. Depending on what we have come through in our lives, our reasons for procrastinating or putting off things for the future (near or distant future) are again different.

In this chapter, we will identify comprehensively what could be the reasons for procrastination by people, generally. It may be the case that some of the reasons you would relate to more precisely, and some reasons may sound silly to you. But, as I said, I repeat, I am trying to holistically cover the possible reasons for procrastination by a different set of people.

Such people may be in full-time jobs or part-time jobs. Some may be entrepreneurs, a solopreneur, professionals like engineers, doctors, lawyers, architects and so on. Also, some may be working moms or a stay-at-home parent. So, bear with me, even if you find a couple of reasons which can be attributable to your cause of procrastination that is enough for you to move to the further section of this book (which is the meaty stuff, i.e., how to kill that procrastination beast).

Okay now, let's get going with a list of different reasons, which I have heard about, and experienced some of them myself, through my own sweat and blood. You may read on to see which one you closely relate to yourself.

Here you go.

1. Fear of Failure

It is the first and foremost reason for people to put off even the most important activities of their lives. This reason alone accounts for a substantial number of people not taking any further action. This fear appears to people to be such a stigma as if failure would mean that it would be a direct question mark on their capabilities.

People tend to think that if they take some action and not succeed in that action, it would mean that there is something wrong with them. Such people want guaranteed returns, i.e., guaranteed success before they are ready to put in any efforts into some project. But there is a well-known principle of life:

No risk = no returns.
Or

Lower the risk = lower the return.

Such people would prefer to keep their funds in the fixed deposit account in their bank, rather than to invest in securities (which entail risk but rewards too). This is the safest place for them and therefore offers the least returns on the investment (because of least quantum of risk involved). Therefore, due to this fear of failure, people in this category rather choose to stay at wherever they are instead of moving forward and taking any action. They feel safe in their current circumstances, but there is a cost for that, i.e., no progress and no real growth in life.

Though I am getting tempted to offer the solutions to this problem here, only, however, as this section of the book talks about only the reasons for procrastination, it would be digressing to touch the solution part in this chapter. Therefore, in order to maintain the preciseness of the chapter, I would simply state the "WHYs" in this section, and we will touch about the "HOWs" in the subsequent sections of this book.

Okay, let's move to the next one.

2. Fear of Success

Some of you may find this quite absurd. I also found this thinking unbelievable until I listened to the audiobook "The Big Leap - Conquer Your Hidden Fear and Take Life to the Next Level" by Gay Hendricks, where he explained about a thing called Upper Limit Problem (ULP in short form). I realized that most of the population suffer from this ULP in one form or another. Let's try to understand this by way of an example:

When we are very happy in a particular situation, enjoying some great moment with our family or friends, suddenly, it happens that we get engaged in an argument with that loved one. Why does this happen?

Hendricks has explained that each of us has an internal barometer of all the emotions, which has set the limit up to which we can experience any emotions (the limits fixed by our minds only). Therefore, when we reach the peak limits of any such emotion of happiness or joy, our minds start giving us a signal that we are not entitled beyond that specified limit. It triggers us to take such action, which has the effect of reducing the level of that emotion, to bring it up to your setup limits of those levels.

Some of you may relate to another example.

Assume you are at level X while measuring your financial status. Honestly, ask yourself now. Do you think that you are entitled to 2X or 3X of your current level of income?

I am sure only a very few people would be able to answer in the affirmative.

I have crossed that stage myself, where the maximum we could think of, in the rise in the level of income per year is around 20% or so, or a very good case being 50% if we switch from one job to another. Similarly, if you are in your own business, profession or doing something of your own, it would be difficult for you to fathom the thought of 2X or 3X of your current level of income. What is all this?

This is called the 'fear of success.'

Now you would try to rationalize it by saying that one has to be practical and look at the ground realities. I have the answer and some good examples too.

The answer is that all rationalization is BS (bullsh*t) and it is just a game your mind plays with you all the time. The reason is, when you are busy with your mind buying such petty arguments; the game changes are already on the job to change the world and their own lives along with it. The world is filled with tons of such examples who have thought 10X of their existing situation and have got 100X of what they are now.

And you, bloody hell, are talking about only a meager 20% of your current situation. Congratulate your mean mind, as it is again winning its game of fooling you one more time. But it is you who has to think now if you want to keep on procrastinating your true success or dream life, or if you want to come out from your self-created upper limit problem.

Sorry for the harsh language, but believe me, I have talked to myself sometimes about this language, and this has worked wonders. I would urge you to thrash your mind, the way you like and you will get rewarded soon with a different result in your life. To put it succinctly, the fear of going beyond our own ULP is something which keeps us restricted up to a certain limit.

If we think, we are about to exceed that ULP, then we sub-consciously start procrastinating the necessary activities required, which has the potential to help us cross that ULP.

3. Fear of What People Will Say

This is another dreaded fear which cripples most of the population, rather it drags the person backward – forget about any progress. And this is my favorite one too (I am even thinking of writing a full book on this, drop me an email at sombathla@gmail.com if you would support this book idea).

In fact, I have personally been plagued with this disease for so many years. If you have noted, my first book "The 30 Hour Day" was published in November 2014, but I chose not to promote my book even at my social network (except my close relatives). Any guesses, why it was that way?

Only because of the fear of what will people think (though now it looks a bit strange to me). I had been a corporate lawyer in my career, and I used to think people would expect something on the legal subjects and topics from me and not a blog or book on the personal development or growth or something.

In fact, the fear is not unfounded. I have a personal example which supports this fear. It is when "The 30 Hour Day" touched the #1 Amazon bestsellers in the time management category and I told a friend about this achievement. But he, in the very first place said, *"But you are a lawyer, and the topics like productivity and personal development are related to human resource only, so why I was writing that in first place"*. Though, he congratulated me after that. But yes, he was successful in affirming my fear of "*what will people say*."

This fear alone infected me enough to keep procrastinating to open up for years. This fear seems so large as if it is a question of one's life or death and therefore appears to be a big enough reason for procrastinating on your big dreams. But lately, I realized this when I stumbled upon the principle of 18:40:60, which was very helpful for me to show up and put up myself openly in this world (see my honest admission to the world at www.sombathla.com). I already covered this 18:40:60 principle in my recent book "Master your Day- Design Your Life."

Precisely, the rule of 18:40: 60 states that human beings think about "what others think about him or her" from a very different perspective at different stages of their lives.

Precisely, the rule signifies:

- When you're 18, you worry about what the world is thinking about you.
- When you're 40, you don't give a darn what anybody thinks about you; and

- Finally, when you're 60, you realize nobody's been thinking about you at all.

But, the rewards of killing this fear are immense, one reward, which @Gary Vaynerchuk has stated is as below:

"When you get rid of what others will think about you, you give yourself the Gift of Speed" Gary Vaynerchuk

You can see the procrastination beast thrown and lying in the dust, once you get rid of this fear of people's view of you.

So, why waste time and live a fabricated life based on what other people think about you?

4. Fear of Losing Comfort Zone

Another significant reason why people keep on deferring taking action on their dreams is that it requires getting out of their comfort zone.

"A comfort zone is a really beautiful place, but nothing grows there"~ Anonymous

You would agree that taking any kind of action towards your goals or dreams is precisely asking you to come out of your comfort zone. It warrants you to show yourself up to the world (your world could be very limited, i.e., only your boss or subordinates or your fellow workers or it may be the entire world).

For most people have a strongly imbibed belief that there is too much pain and suffering if they move out of their comfort zone. But the irony is that the majority of the population is not even in the comfort zone. The day to day life is not a comfortable one. See the people around, waking up early, rushing for their work, reaching home late at night, with no time to have some cheerful moments to cherish. But despite that, people don't tend to take some serious action to address the situation. Do you know why it is so?

Because most people think that:

"A known devil is better than an unknown Angel"~ Anonymous

Their comfort zone is "a known devil" because they can foresee or predict what a known devil does. Surprising, Isn't it?

And that's why they stop, then and there. They make their comfort zone in such uncomfortable situations only because of familiarity. Being familiar with the outcomes of their day to day activities gives a sense of certainty to most of the people. This sense of certainty of outcome, even if the outcome is burdensome, is still acceptable to most of us, because it keeps us guarded against some unknown or uncertain future.

Please try to understand that human mind is a lazy creature by default and tends to work less (though it wants to get more out of least efforts). But there are no free lunches, as they say. People are busy applauding the events, but the process, which leads to any mega event, is an arduous task. It requires more frequent coming out of comfort zones. The successful people know that staying in the comfort zone is the riskiest place to be in because that will make them stagnant. They know that:

"Iron rusts without use, stagnant water rots or freezes in the cold and the human mind withers likewise"~ Leonardo Da Vinci

They also believe that:

"Life begins at the end of comfort zone"~ Neale Donald Walsh

So, if you are too stuck in your comfort zone, then there is bound to be a tendency to procrastinate in any action which leads you to your dreams.

5. Low or No Confidence in Success

The beliefs gifted to us by our society and thanks to our innocent reinforcement of such beliefs in our minds, most of us have very well cemented this most non-resourceful neuro pathway in our brains. Most of the population believes that success is something which is for others and we can only applaud such events. But when it comes to imagining or visualizing our success, our old thinking patterns and non-resourceful beliefs stand tall in front of us and start shouting at us, something like this:

- Who are you to achieve this?
- Did you see your past and what significant thing you have done so far?
- What makes you think of these things, as you don't have a required skill set?

This radio station broadcast in our heads is good enough to beat our confidence, and we start to procrastinate, taking action on our dearest of dreams and ambitions. This is because it gives us comfort to be a part of the bigger mass, as it makes us feel secure as a part of the crowd. Society does not want people to succeed. You name any successful person on this planet, who was not ridiculed and made fun of when starting out something big?

And for most of the people starting something different or thinking bigger than the reasonable one from society's point of view, it is a big and daunting task. It requires tons of confidence to go against the wind. The majority of the population stays miserable with low or no confidence in their own abilities to touch the higher limits.

"Negative and toxic people will drag you down with their insults, criticisms, and put-downs. Try not to stoop to their level. It is their own insecurities that drive their behavior, and it has nothing to do with you. Move on and away from that negativity" ~Anonymous.

It is but natural that if one is plagued with low or no confidence disease, then he or she will continue to procrastinate on the most important activities of his or her life.

6. Perfectionist Syndrome

Few people procrastinate due to their inner desire of being a perfectionist in whatever they do. Such people do not want to sound stupid if there is a minor comma or typo error in their article. They have a thinking pattern that even a small error in their work will make them appear careless or unprofessional. Such thinking pattern has the effect of delaying the release of your 95% completed work to whosoever it needs to go. Only for the last 5% of the work, which I believe in most cases goes unnoticed by the recipients, such set of people keeps on deferring the delivery of the work further.

There is a very good blog article by Seth Godin on the importance of shipping, which categorically touches upon this aspect. Seth states that:

> *Shipping is fraught with risk and danger.*
>
> *Every time you raise your hand, send an email, launch a product or make a suggestion, you're exposing yourself to criticism. Not just criticism, but the negative consequences that come with wasting money, annoying someone in power or making a fool of yourself.*
>
> *It's no wonder we're afraid to ship.*

It's not clear you have much choice, though. A life spent curled in a ball, hiding in the corner might seem less risky, but in fact, it's certain to lead to ennui and eventually failure.

Since you're going to ship anyway, then, the question is: why bother indulging your fear?

In a long-distance race, everyone gets tired. The winner is the runner who figures out where to put the tired, figures out how to store it away until after the race is over. Sure, he's tired.

Everyone is. That's not the point. The point is to run.

The Same thing is true for shipping, I think. Everyone is afraid. Where do you put the fear?

The preceding excerpt is hitting the nail bang on the head. A person with the perfectionism syndrome is a chronic procrastinator. Anything less than perfect and thinking of shipping it becomes a question of life and death for the procrastinator.

So, the simple choice, until this is done perfectly, makes a procrastinator sound like a super intellectual, who doesn't want to do injustice with the world by sharing a minuscule less than perfect product. Until this fellow gets rids of this syndrome, moving ahead to raise his voice, share his opinion or deliver his product is really a nightmare for him. Rest assured, you will get to know some strategies to overcome this precise issue in the next chapter.

7. Instant Gratification Syndrome

It is now a fact that our minds prefer to experience the feeling of instant gratification rather than focusing on the long-term rewards. Until there is a real urgency for some activities, our minds prefer to have a feeling of instant gratification over a long-term reward. The sole reason for this is that we cannot see the long-term reward clearly as compared to the short-term instant feeling of joy.

It could be:

- Choosing to gossip over a cup of coffee with a colleague rather focus and finish a presentation for a client next week.

- Preferring to sit on a couch to watch a latest Netflix movie rather than to hit the gym- the reward of watching a movie is instant, while the benefits of fitness will only appear only after some time.

In the previous chapters, you have already gotten into the details of this instant gratification monkey in our minds. You already know that this monkey gets to its job, only when a 'panic monster' thumps on its door. Until then, instant gratification monkey prefers to stay in its gaga land. Since we already talked a lot about this instant gratification in the introduction chapter and also in the mindset chapter, it does not require further elaboration. This is briefly captured here, as it forms part of the key reasons for procrastination.

8. Digital Distractions

Let's admit this. Even the people claiming themselves to be more productive are unable to escape from the widespread encroachment of social media of our minds. There are tons of social media platforms flourishing these days. Facebooks, Twitters, Instagrams of the world have already caught the maximum attention span of most of us. On the top of it, a lot more new developments are still in the offing.

The notification tones or the alerts on our smartphones are very difficult to avoid, and it requires a huge quantum of self-discipline not to get distracted from our productivity zone. So, in the middle of doing some high leverage activity work, suddenly you find some tweet or post from your network, and you find it very difficult to hold on your craving till you have finished your key work. This is more of an emotional discipline issue. You have all the feelings of guilt, anger, fear or others popping in your head, which stimulates our intentions to leave everything in between and immediately address the emotional craving.

Take an example:

You receive a Facebook notification, in which one of your acquaintances is sharing his/her opinion on any wider public issue, which is not in line with your ideology. You know that this Facebook notification is not at all related to the important work, you are carrying on currently. But you chose to get distracted and immediately starting thumping keys on FB and don't stop until you release your ideological fart from your mind. Then you re-start focusing on your most important task. With this kind of indiscipline in our daily routines, procrastinating on the most important activities is the natural outcome.

We will cover in detail the practical action steps on how to address this in the next chapter on strategies to beat the procrastination monster.

9. Boring Task

Most of the time, the monotonous nature of our work drives us nuts and prompts us to push away from even our most rewarding projects. Our minds are designed to seek novelty. That is the reason that we always crave a different kind of food. We always want to go on vacation at different places. Also, we want to have a different kind of adventure in our lives.

Therefore, if the nature of work performed by you has become monotonous or routine, and it does not pump you up to jump into the action, you will try to procrastinate on the work as much as possible. You will do the work only when it becomes an urgent and unavoidable work, and the cost of procrastination is much higher.

This all happens due to the instant gratification monkey, which wants fun and joy every time, even at the cost of our important value-generating activities. But there is a solution to that as well. We covered a few examples already in the previous chapter under the heading "instant gratification monkey." But anyways, you will find more strategies to beat procrastination, which arises on this count.

10. Difficult task

While the boring task is on the one extreme (i.e., mundane activity requiring lesser intellectual efforts), the complex nature of the work stands tall on the other extreme. Therefore, if the nature of work to be performed is a complex task seeking the much bigger involvement of your mind, energy and time, you would continue to pull back. The excuses for not doing it could be something like this:

- It is already a half day overdue because of other urgent activities;
- I could not start my X work so far. Therefore, let me defer the work till next day morning or sometime later, so I can do when I have more mental or physical energy (except for the few times of genuine cases, mostly this is an excuse for procrastination).
- I am confused whether I should do it myself or try to delegate this work further.
- I am not sure if I am capable of doing this work at all.
- I have never done this before such difficult task, and I am not 100%

sure that I would be able to deliver it
in time.

Therefore, we tend to procrastinate on such
seemingly difficult tasks for next best time,
when we would be in our state full of
energy. We tend to fill in our day with all
sorts of non-significant but mundane
activities, just to stay busy. We tend to keep
ourselves busy with various chores, only to
avoid taking action on our key priorities,
which we have categorized as complex
tasks.

Stay tuned to understand few more key
reasons for procrastination and then we
will get into all strategies and tactics for
killing this procrastination monster to
boost our productivity.

11. Overwhelming Work

Another reason why we do procrastinate is
that sometimes, it appears that we have too
much on our plates to handle. We have so
many tasks lined up that it seems very
difficult to make a choice as to which
activity to start and which to hold back.
Such feeling leaves us in the lurch and even

makes us handicapped to decide anything. But bear in mind that how much importance you give to that little noise in your head to procrastinate and don't do the work, the ultimate truth is that it is only you who has to decide the way to finally handle that work.

I understand that most of the people with the feeling of being overwhelmed treat themselves as victims rather in the driver's seat. We start blaming the circumstances, outside environment, people, for everything, which makes us feel overwhelmed by the mere volume of the work. Unfortunately, the more we sit on the side, plagued by inaction, the problem of procrastination deepens its roots in our heads leading to further dismay and stress in our lives. Because as is rightly said:

"It is in the moments of your indecision that your dreams are destroyed"~ Dr. Mark Dussault

Okay, so now we have covered substantially why people procrastinate due to different kinds of reasons. Also, you would have listed your reasons for procrastination of your important activities (if you do procrastinate). You could have one or many reasons out of the above listed.

The next chapter is a panacea for this disease, regardless of whatever symptoms you have or whatever mindset bug, you are suffering from. So, let's jump straight into the most useful action-oriented chapter of this book.

****

CHAPTER 6: 27 PROVEN TACTICS TO CONQUER PROCRASTINATION AND GET THINGS DONE

****

"Procrastination is like a credit card: It's lot of fun until you get the bill"~Christopher Parker

Congratulations!
You have come a long way in your journey of exploration to resolve the procrastination problem. The best part is that before this chapter, you have already understood clearly what exactly what procrastination is and how it is different from prioritization and procrastination on purpose. You now know the Procrastinators Code; which procrastinators use to justify their inaction.

You didn't stop there, as you have also peeped inside the minds of a procrastinator and non-procrastinator and understood the fine distinction between how these two different Mind operating systems work. Finally, in the last chapter, you have also gone through the comprehensive list of reasons as to why you procrastinate.

Great, we covered a lot. I am happy about it and have a subtle feeling that you would be feeling that way too. (But, I can only know about that through your honest reviews. You know, reviews are gold to the authors, so please put your reviews at Amazon.com after reading the book.)

Wonderful, so let's keep the momentum on. In other words, the "Iron is Hot" now, and whatever shape you want to give it, that's possible. I believe, with all this understanding, you are standing at the right juncture, where you can easily implement various strategies to the deeper levels of your mind. The key benefit is that now it would be difficult for you to digress and rather procrastinate in implementing these strategies in your life.

It is important to remember the key is the application of the acquired knowledge.

"Knowledge is useless without consistent application"~ Julian Hall

So, without further ado, let's keep moving, as we still have a lot to cover:
Here you go...

1: 5 Minutes Rule

This rule is a sort of 'appetizer' for your work, just like you have some light snacks before starting your main-course dinner☺. So how does this appetizer for any of our actions work to beat the procrastination monster?

First and foremost, it is a technique to trick your mind gradually (sometimes you have to trick your mind, instead of every time getting tricked by it, right?). Under this rule, you have to convince your mind to just stick to that cumbersome, burdensome, slothful, filthy appearing, mundane (or whatever you feel about it) activity for only 5 minutes. You can tell your mind in advance that you will do that activity only for 5 minutes and then you may leave it. But you will now ask:

If you can leave after 5 minutes for sure, then how will you get the work done? A logical observation! Just like 2+2=4, right? But try to understand that we are dealing with a complex creation of God called "MIND," which doesn't work on mathematics or logic, rather it works on its emotions and feelings most of the time.

If our minds had been working solely on the logic, all these advertising agencies would have shut their shops already. This is because human psychology prompts our mind to make decisions based on emotions of fear, greed, lust, etc. So, psychology plays far more of a role than the logical brain in most of our decisions. Okay, you would say, and then come back to the question:

But then how does the 5 minutes rule help us to get our work done, although we don't feel like doing it?

The way it works is that in those 5 minutes of that activity, you exercise the pre-frontal cortex portion of your brain (front portion of your brain). Unless you already know, the pre-frontal cortex is responsible for all our learning. It is the portion, which applies all its willpower and energy for the learning anything complex. It is responsible for handling all complex activities, be it learning a new language, working on a very complicated advisory work or handling any other kind of project, which involves huge processes into it.

But, the key quality of this portion of the brain is that it wants to quicklu shift the work on an automated basis. That automated portion of the brain is the subconscious mind (which is located on the lower back side of our skull), which seemingly makes the thing happen on an automated basis, like riding a bicycle, driving a car or the simplest activity like brushing your teeth on an autopilot basis.

So, the 5 minutes time, which you put on an activity, which you don't want to do (but which is very significant for your career) is the exercise given to your pre-frontal cortex. In that 5 minutes time, there is a possibility that if your mind honestly gets into it, it starts to get engaged in it. No guarantee that it will happen every time, but the chances are that you may get into a state of flow and stay there longer.

Also, since the mind works on the emotions, there is a possibility that when 5 minutes within the work, your emotions get changed. Maybe you start seeing the rewards coming out of the completion of that activity. Maybe you see the adverse impact on your career, health or relationship or personal life if you don't spend time on the chosen activity.

A lot of times, I have succeeded in convincing myself in hitting the gym, with an initial promise of shorter time. I just tell my mind that I would just do five minutes of treadmill or cycling or cross fit exercise and if I don't like it, then I will say bye for the day. But I have noted that around 7-8 times out of 10, I have been able to continue much longer, as I have started liking the process and enjoyed staying longer (change of emotions), as I felt the benefit of good health and fit body after that (foresight of a future reward).

I have experimented this with my writing (which is not always very exciting stuff, believe me!) and this 5 minutes rule has worked well for me. Therefore, the same should apply to any of your activity (which you don't want to do and defer it to tomorrow).

I am sure; you can also find some examples of change in emotions, before starting work (which you didn't want) and later when you are into that work. It is worth experimenting with keeping your logical procrastination-loving brain aside for 5 minutes.

2: Calendar is the King & Deadlines Keep You Moving

Remember your childhood days or anytime in your school or college education? You knew the dates of examinations, as these are decided and announced in advance. Therefore, you were already aware what exam you had to take on a particular day. How did that help?

It frequently helped us to revisit and plan our studies better. Even most of the master procrastinators had to get their butt in the chair in the face of a calendar deadline.

Assume there were no dates announced and you simply had to keep on studying and one fine day you would take your exam.

Seems absurd, right? Even it seems funny.

Take another example of your workplace or career. You had been told in advance of a board meeting or an important investors meeting or any production planning schedule or any significant client meeting. You would obviously expect prior timelines so that you could plan and execute the necessary preparatory steps to better deliver on the given date.

Here again, assume you were told to keep preparing and one fine day, you would suddenly be thrown, with your half-prepared presentation slides, into the boardroom or meeting with the key client. How would you feel?

Chances are you would be there with half-baked information or even blank in some cases. Some of you might even ridicule such chaos openly. Because you find it totally unreasonable, right?

Again, it would seem totally haphazard. You would feel rather frustrated, no?

But, now with the same thought train going on, ask yourself, 'do we put our life priorities or dreams on any of the calendars? Do we assign any deadlines for important meetings with ourselves? Let's make a clear distinction here.

We want others to put the priorities on the calendar and show the deadlines. We want others to decide the repercussions of not adhering to the timelines. But we don't want ourselves to be self-disciplined in our life priorities.

So, you must have some own personal priorities.

- It could be losing 20 pounds in next six months.
- It could be looking for that adventure mountain hiking to wake up your inner youth.
- It could be planning an exotic vacation with your family or friends to your dream destination.

Here we are talking about the activities, which. though are important, but there is no timeline or deadline put on those by us. For want of deadlines, such important activities, in any area of your life, keep on getting postponed to <u>a never coming tomorrow</u>.

Take your example of an adventure trip for mountain tracking, which you had been planning for years. Why don't you put that on the calendar and make that as a deadline to achieve?

Have you been engrossed in mortgages and living pay-check to pay-check every month after month? Why don't you considering looking for another better paying job or start a new side business or a venture to help you earn extra money?

Put a date on your calendar for brainstorming these activities and schedule a deadline for achieving those. If you don't put them on the calendar, you will tend to defer them in most cases, as there is no sense of urgency there.

How does the calendar work?

The putting in your calendar reminds you of taking immediate action on that listed item. It puts the deadlines for the action to be taken very much in advance. For example, I have already put on my calendar the timelines to release this very book tentatively in the second week of August 2017. At the max, what may happen is that I might achieve 90% of my set target, i.e., may delay the release by a week or so (because I don't see an immediate and instant loss if I somehow miss the deadline). Putting something on your calendar to take action on the activity and assigning a deadline to complete the activity generates positive emotions. It makes you feel alive that you are working towards a clear objective of yours. If there is no objective goal with a marked deadline, you tend to be dragging the things much longer. You should remember the below quote:

"Always shoot for the moon, even if you miss, you will land amongst stars" ~Les Brown

To sum up, unless there is a sense of urgency in any action, you will keep on dragging it to some future date, which is a never arriving tomorrow. Make the best use of your calendar and deadlines to move you forward for achieving bigger dreams and goals of yours.

3: Forget Perfectionism-Excellence works Better

That is my favorite one, as I can relate it to my personal experience. I might be sharing lots of my personal examples here. Just to be very honest, this is not to brag about that I am in any manner great and have already overcome this obstacle. Rather this is to deeply connect with you, my esteemed reader, so that you can relate the experience with some of your own life experience and imbibe the same deeply in your mind.

"Words are how we think; stories are how we link"~ Christina Baldwin

I am allowing my inner self to come out and share another story with you. I wouldn't have published either of my previous books, had I chosen to remain infected by the perfectionism bug any longer. Though I procrastinated it only for a couple of weeks during my first book, under the guise that I needed to make it perfect. Fortunately, and I am grateful to God that it was only a few weeks, but you would have seen people waiting much longer to come out with their best product or deliverable.

Perfectionism means waiting endlessly to put out your work to your world in the fear that there might be some minor lapse or lacuna here and there. It is waiting to make your work totally flawless; else you have a fear of getting criticism from people in your surrounding or network. Let me be very clear here. I am not in any manner advocating for doing crap work, which will be disastrous for your career and life in general.

What I am suggesting here is that you should work your butt off to create an excellent work. Yes, yours and my mission are to promote the excellence (but not perfection). In fact, there is nothing perfect in this world. And the excellence comes by consistent action and then taking consistent feedback from the outcomes. A beautiful quote below will clarify the point:

"I am careful not to confuse excellence with perfection. Excellence, I can reach for; Perfection is God's business"~ Michael J. Fox

But your next obvious question would be, as to when you should be comfortable to make a judgment that your work is crafted well and is ready to go out to your world. Here, to avoid writing it again, I am simply taking the excerpts from my previous book "The 30- Hour Day, where I had explained categorically, as to when you should feel comfortable that your product is ready for putting out to the world.

> *"Shipment is the key. Release the email, which is pending with you for endless research (not a giant life-changing, risk–it-all-venture) today, and you can feel the sense of relaxation and fulfillment. Believe me, the initial fear and doubts about yourself will start vanishing, after you start doing it on a faster basis.*

> *The key question that arises here is when can you comfortably*

determine that it is 90-95 % done? And the reasonable answer to that is after you followed the steps stated below. If you have completed the following steps in your work, then you would be in a safer position to deliver it.

1. Whatever your knowledge you have about the subject, you have already utilized it.

2. You have done web research on the subject and read the available relevant material.

3. If you have a colleague working with you or under you, you have taken their views on the same, and there is no disagreement.

4. If you are surrounded by experts and the situation warrants that you have completed preliminary informal discussions with them (the experts could be your friends, or it could be consultants, which you already use for your work).

So, when you have done all of the above, there is simply no need to keep waiting endlessly due to your "perfectionist mindset."

I believe that this works for most of the activities done by you (I use this), though some very high-stake issues may need some extra diligence, i.e., detailed expert advice (but not all decisions in your work could be like this)."

The moot point here is that perfectionism is an excuse, which tends to come under the innocent facade that you want to deliver only the greatest work of yours. You simply need to follow the above-stated technique and get rid of this sickness as soon as you can. You don't need to wait for any sermons from God or seek any specific permission from anyone to start acting; you can do it now.

However, if you think you need any permission to show your excellence out to the world, I at this moment grant you that permission! (no offense, just a way to nudge you a bit).

"You don't have to be great to start, but you have to start to be great"~Zig Ziglar

4: Accountability Partner Rocks (rocks you!)

Fortunately, or unfortunately, you and I have only one mind, and that's also a very strange one.

You must have come across endless instances, wherein one fine morning, you were fully geared up to jump straight into action for any given goal or objective of yours. You had planned the required action steps to achieve that goal. But suddenly as you pass through your day and by the evening, you start to feel an urge to postpone that activity. In a moment, out of the blue moon, you start doubting your decision. The enthusiasm of the morning starts seeming much too optimistic and somehow unrealistic to achieve. Why does this happen?

Don't get surprised. The mind is an animal like this only and needs to be tamed and trained consistently. You and I know very clearly that whatever we consistently think about we become that only. Therefore, we need to bring consistency to our thought patterns.

Here comes the role of an accountability partner to our rescue. Your accountability partner holds you accountable for your action on a day to day basis. It hangs a stick on your head and reminds you if you start getting influenced by negativity bugs of your mind.

You know, unless we become the complete masters of our mind, which is a stage of nirvana or totally an enlightened Buddha, we would need a lot of discipline in pushing ourselves forward towards our goals.

That's why the best of the best sportspersons believe in engaging a coach. Coaches are not in any manner better or superior to the players, but they are better observers, and they have an independent, unbiased view towards any situation.

Another best way to have an accountability partner is through masterminding. Some of you may be aware of the concept of masterminding. This concept was coined by Napoleon Hill in his famous book "Think and Grow Rich." I have explained the concept of masterminding in detail in my other book titled "Master Your Day- Design Your life" if you wish to get much deeper into it. However, just for a quick reference, it can be explained as below:

Mastermind is nothing but joining hands and minds with people, who are like-minded so that they all can learn from each other and also brainstorm the growth possibilities together. The members of the mastermind group hold each other accountable for the deliverables expected from others.

If you cannot afford or you don't wish to start directly with a coach or a mastermind group, no worries, you can start this directly with one of your best friends or your spouse or any other relative. Both of you can share with each other your growth journey and hold the other person accountable if the activity put on your respective list is not completed within time.

So, how engaging an accountability partner helps in curbing procrastination?

As human beings, we want to avoid pain and maximize the pleasure. I would re-emphasize that whole human psychology and all human actions are solely influenced by one simple formula and that is "*Avoid the pain and maximize the pleasure.*" I bet if you choose any of your actions; the sole underlying principle would be this only. So how it is relevant here?

Yes, it is. If you have promised to take certain action in a given timeline, your accountability partner may be your coach or your mastermind group member or anyone else; you would want to avoid the 'pain' of the embarrassment of not meeting the deadlines. You would want to avoid the 'pain' of being rejected or ridiculed for not keeping your words.

In fact, our bosses or anyone to whom we are accountable are our accountability partners, although you might treat them as if forced upon on. We are going one step further here to beat the procrastination monster to voluntarily engage the accountability partners for taking actions on the significant stuff of our lives.

Therefore, if someone holds us accountable towards our promised actions, we tend to work on those deliverables to avoid any embarrassment. Therefore, any instincts to procrastinate on your work, immediately reminds you of the pain of the loss of your credibility or goodwill, so you better prefer to take action. You can beat the procrastination by this way.

5: Visualize your Future, if You Don't Change Yourself

I am totally convinced that if you are reading this book or read any other kind of productivity enhancement book, you are very sincere about your bright future. So, you must be imagining or visualizing your future, your dreams, and your ambition positively.

Under the current strategy, you have to assess how far you are from your visualized future, by comparing it with the current situation you are in. We all know goal setting very well, right?

Achievement of the goal is nothing but travel from the current situation to a different and always a better destination. In fact, it is a journey from Point A to Point B, and in this journey, everyone is unsure whether it would be a smooth ride or it is going to be a topsy-turvy bumpy ride. Therefore, if you are clear about what action or steps are required for traveling your success journey from point A to point B, then why would you stop taking the necessary action or why would you delay or postpone those necessary actions.

Here, you need to be thoughtful and convince your mind that any delay, deferment or any other form of procrastination is nothing but the postponement of your dreamed or visualized future. You have to viscerally show your mind the repercussions and the adverse ramifications in the form of the undesirable future of yourself if you don't stick to your priorities and schedule.

You have to threaten your mind about your sinking into the mud of mediocrity if you don't act as per your plan to achieve your dreams. You have to show your mind again and again that if you stay acting as per your current way, then it is not going to help you to achieve your dreams or goals in the time to come. If your mind continues to repeat its old pattern of procrastinating and avoid taking action, then you should even insult your mind by saying it is "Insane" because:

"Insanity is doing the same thing over and over again and expecting different results" ~ Albert Einstein

Therefore, one of the best ways to kill the procrastination is to scare your mind that you are not going to achieve or delay the achievement of your dreams if you don't go as per your planned action steps. The idea is to realize your mind about the future pain of not being able to fulfill your dreams.

6: Obstacle is the way- Plan in Advance

In his best-selling book "*Obstacle Is The Way*," the author, Ryan Holiday has chosen the title of the book as a very bold statement. He goes on to elaborate that in our journey towards any of our goals, the one thing which is bound to come surely is "**obstacles**." They can be in any form. They could be your physical challenges, financial limitations, relationships holding you back, or emotionally draining experience. It could be anything. But, yes, it is sure that they are bound to come.

Also, Randy Pausch very rightly stated:

"The brick walls are there for a reason. The brick walls are not there to keep us out. The brick walls are there to give us a chance to show how badly we want something."

But it is the natural reaction of most of the living world that they start feeling overwhelmed when they come across a plethora of new developments in their journey, and they call it obstacles. Again, it seems obvious for most people to feel stressed when you are not able to figure out the next steps. It happens that while going to an uncharted area (which might be your beacon towards growth) you are not sure about what might come in your way.

But, you can test it out that in the depth of your heart, there is a belief that even though you are not able to foresee your path clearly, but there is definitely a way from your existing situation to your dream situation (because you have seen people touching those goals already). Let's try to understand this by way of an example.

Assume you are riding in a helicopter or airplane. You can take an aerial view of the ground situation. Here you can see better the distance from point A to point B of your journey. You can see the big rocks, topsy-turvy path, mountain areas, and some forest area and so on. But you can also see the end point, i.e., point B, which is your destination.

But unfortunately, if you have not taken the aerial view and are moving on the ground, then you probably are not well conversant with roadblocks, which will come in the way. So, you might start thinking that probably there is no destination across these roadblocks. You might start getting skeptical that might be there are endless struggles on the way, or probably, the route you have taken is the wrong one. You may start thinking to stop and procrastinate taking any further steps.

There are two kinds of people. One, who as soon as they hit the roadblock or any steep or any shallow on the way, they get scared and anxious, they start validating their fears. They start validating what their close relatives, father, mother or spouse has already told them. Their loud sound starts budging in your head. *"We told you that this is not going to work, play safe, travel lesser and safer and leave that distant dream to be achieved by someone else."*

Then, there is another set of people; I call them soldiers. Now when these soldiers find an obstacle in their way, they immediately say, Hmmm, yes, I was expecting you and now will figure out how to cross you. In other words, this category of people plans for their obstacles well in advance. So, in the very first place, they know that obstacles are bound to come, so they are not surprised, neither are they frightened or frustrated. But they are expectant of the obstacles and have accordingly put on the relevant safety jackets, helmets, etc. to cope up with the situations.

But how do they plan in advance?
They do enough research about how the journey is going to be and what tools are required to safely travel the path (i.e., they have understood the aerial view of the situation already). They read a lot of the people who have already traveled that path and know the experience of such well-traveled persons. Because they believe that:

"Success leaves clue" ~ Tony Robbins

Don't you read and research a lot, when you are planning your vacation? Don't you look at the features of hotels to stay in, i.e., safety, convenience, etc.? Don't you check the risky places in the other town, which you must avoid, to avoid spoiling your trip? Don't you ask your friend, who has gone for mountain tracks in the last vacation, for tips? Don't you check what best route he or she had taken?

Surely, you would check with him, what kind of tools and equipment he has carried with him or her. You also would check with him or her the emergency situations and how to handle that. So, you agree that you do a lot of research on your own while planning your trips.

Also, they do take advice from seasoned people, who have already traveled the less trodden path. They are always ready to seek help and not filled with shallow ego, i.e., they don't assume that they know all the answers. They believe in the rule below:

"Learn from the mistake of others. You can't live long enough to make them all yourself" ~Eleanor Roosevelt

Therefore, if the reason for your procrastination is merely the volume of obstacles or due to the feeling of being overwhelmed. then you should follow the above strategy. You should plan for all obstacles which might come your way even before you start. This way, you would not stop and procrastinate to take action, as you already had known about the obstacles and you also researched how to tackle these obstacles.

7: Eat That Frog

In his best-selling book, "Eat that Frog," Brian Tracy has advised that the very first thing in the morning should be eating that ugliest frog. He explains that frog means your difficult but high-value activity, which if done, will be a significant achievement for the day and other activities will seem comparatively of lesser importance.

In my author journey, one of the hardest parts is being creative and writing a massive number of words on the paper. Of course, reaching to the masses is another important activity, but you must have the best product, you believe in before you reach out to the world.

I have personally chosen for myself to write specified numbers of hours or a specified number of words per day daily, first thing in the morning. After writing for dedicated period or words, there comes a sense of satisfaction that now I have handled one of the toughest and most important tasks; I can work very smoothly on the other projects.

Take a reverse example. You keep yourself busy since morning in the mundane activities, which are not high value or high leverage activities and did not work on your main objective activity. Now, you see, it is already the middle of the day! What will happen now?

Now, in this latter part of your day, you will already start feeling exhausted and at a loss of energy. So, you won't be able to focus on your "Frog" or your key activity and thus not be able to progress in your projects.

A procrastinator needs to tell his mind and tell him the rewards of completing the most difficult task in the top priority. This is because, in the earlier part of the day, the mind has more energy and will-power to get into anything difficult, if it is pushed to do that. The better energy in the morning will help you to overpower the procrastination instinct. Whereas in the later part of the day, the willpower and energy are already depleted significantly, so it is very difficult to dominate the procrastination tactics of our mindset.

Therefore, with utilizing your energy and willpower on most important activities as first things in the day, you would be able to conquer the procrastination instinct.

8: Progress deserves Reward

Human minds love appreciation. In fact, nothing changes from a kid needing attention to a grown-up adult, when it comes to appreciation of the work.

You see that the child expressly communicates his or her unhappiness when his or her achievements are not well appreciated. But the adults, if not appreciated for their actions, show their dissatisfaction differently and one way is to procrastinate taking any further action. We all are wired this way. When we don't get an appreciation for our actions, then there seems no motivation or reward to continue doing the same action.

But we live in a world where everyone is busy in their workload, their own stress and other pressing areas of one's life. So, who has got the time to appreciate or reward the progress attained by you in your work?

I remember a recent incident when one of my acquaintances had put in his resignation paper in his organization. As this guy was performing well, he was obviously called to inquire the reasoning for his leaving. And the honest admission was that he was not enjoying it, as the environment was not conducive to working there. At that junction, the boss told him that she was very happy with the work and even quoted few examples of good work. The employee was surprised that if that was the case, he should have been communicated about the same, which would have made him feel better and motivated. So, the point is that the life works this way only.

Then how do you handle this?

The straightforward answer is that we are the captain of our ships. Our action or inaction should never be dependent on another person's reaction. So next time, whatever small or big progress you do, don't wait for others to react and reward your progress.

Be your own cheerleader and reward yourself. This reward can be instantly in the form of a pat on your shoulder or a round of applause for you for achieving the progress. Or it can be inviting your close friend or family members for a nice dinner out to celebrate your small wins.

You will instantly feel encouraged to continue to work on your projects, with your inbuilt motivation or reward system. By consistent practice, you would become your own cheerleader and would never feel any dependency on outside pumping up to keep you going. That way you become unstoppable, because there is a guarantee in your mind that every time you achieve something, you will be rewarded.

"What you appreciate, appreciates"
~Lynee Twist

9: Pomodoro Technique- Focus Chunking Method

Let me admit frankly; I cannot perform without this technique now. If I try to. I find myself wasting much time, instead of being productive.

This is a very simple technique. If you are in the habit of procrastination, merely because it seems too big to handle in the limited time available to you, this technique is going to help you.

The **Pomodoro Technique** is a time management method developed by Francesco Cirillo in the late 1980s. The technique uses a timer to break down work into intervals, traditionally 25 minutes in length, separated by short breaks.
You have to work in a stretch of 25 minutes with a complete focus and without any distraction, which is followed by a break of 5 minutes. This sequence needs to be followed four times in a row namely 25 minutes of focused work with 5 minutes of rest. After that, you take a longer break of 15 minutes or so.

This 2 hours of work (with breaks sprinkled in between) are the sources of heightened productivity and very helpful to kill the procrastination. Because you know that you have to work on the project for a continuous 25 minutes, consistently, and then you can take a break for 5 minutes. Some of you might be thinking that they may lose the flow of their action if they take such a frequent break in between.

The above may sound counter-intuitive approach.

But no, that is not the case. David Allen in his best-selling book *"Getting Things Done"* has stated that you don't need more time to produce more, rather you need a clearer head. These 5 minutes of break provide a relaxation window, in which your mind can disengage with what one is doing and therefore gets a fresh perspective on the work after the break. And it keeps adding up after each 25-minute stage.

Had you been doing consistently without any break, there is a possibility that you may continue to run faster, but probably, in a wrong direction. You might end up realizing after a stretch of 2 hours that the direction was to be slightly tweaked before getting full throttle in the wrong direction.

This technique is called Pomodoro Technique, and you may simply download a mobile app on your smartphone named "Clockwork Tomato," which is pre-set with 25 minutes time for work and 5 minutes for break and 15 minutes for a longer break. Try this to see a quick solution to your procrastination problem, arising due to overwhelming of the tasks in front of you.

10: Parkinson Principle- You Decide the Time Required

Another very important principle to kill the procrastination monster is to use Parkinson's Law. This principle states that work expands itself by the number of hours allocated for the work. In other words, the lesser the time you earmark for some activity, the more effectively you handle that activity. There is every chance that you would have already experienced this in your real life.

Imagine you had an exam or an interview or a new customer meeting, which is scheduled to be held three weeks later. Suddenly, you get an email or phone call or message that said the event is prescheduled to happen next week. Now, what is your initial reaction (mind it, it will vary from person to person)? It could be a scary feeling or thoughts of frustration, anxiety, etc. on such a sudden change. You might feel overwhelmed with the volume of work still left to be done for that important event.

But in most of the cases, the truth is that if that event is really important and matters for your success, you work pretty hard to address the situation in the shorter timeframe. The key message here is that your mind adapts to the changes and works according to the situation.

Now, the practice step for you is to allocate reasonably stretched timelines to achieve the same goal. This will help you exercise and thus strengthen your mind muscle.

Next time, if you have a feeling to procrastinate certain activities; you should purposefully allocate yourself lesser amount of time to complete that project. You would be surprised at the elasticity of your mind that it can accomplish the same in the lesser amount of time. It is going to be a two-edged sword in your favor. How?

On one side, if you are procrastinating the work merely because it is going to take a longer amount of time, you win, because you are already allotting a lesser amount of time for getting that work done. On the other hand, you get that cumbersome work done in the shorter amount of time. Isn't that great?

Let's move to the next one.

11: Pareto Principle- Small is the Real Big

Without this principle, any kind of discussions on boosting productivity or killing the procrastination is incomplete.

I have referred this principle in my other books as a very helpful tool for enhancement of productivity. This tool is very apt for killing procrastination. Most of the time, we tend to procrastinate due to our internal assessment that this activity does not appear to be that relevant to be taken up immediately. And the good news is that you may be right a few times. You are not supposed to do everything immediately, which comes to your desk, rather certain activities have to be deferred or say, prioritized, given the limited amount of time and resource you have with you.

Pareto Principle or 80:20 principle works on this underlying basis. Below is the excerpt from my previous book "**The 30 Hour Day**" explaining this principle in detail:

"The Pareto principle was formulated after the name of the Italian economist Vilfredo Pareto in 1906. This principle is also known as 80:20 Principle. It simply states that the world works around the principle that only 20% of your activities (even lesser) are as important to deliver to you the 80% results (even more) in your life. It could be substantiated by following facts:

- *99% of the World's wealth is accumulated by only 1% of the people.*
- *80% or more of every business's turnover/profits are contributed by only 20% or less of its customers.*
- *If you satisfy 20% of the people in your life with your work, that will give you an 80% assurance of the perfect working life.*
- *The list can still go on...*

To be productive and effective in discharging your job, you need to watch your to-do list consistently.

You must apply the Pareto principle. You have to scrutinize all the activities and ascertain what 20% of the activities if you invest time on, have the potential to deliver you the 80% of your results."

What is the takeaway for curing the procrastination problem here?

The key takeaway is this. If the activity you are procrastinating is not your 20% activity (which gives your 80% results), then you can, and in fact, you should, procrastinate doing such activities.

For example, in your business, the new client development and the existing client acquisition is 20% activity, which is responsible for 80% of your revenues, then you may choose to procrastinate other 80% activity to be done at a later stage.

However, since you have identified that some activity is your 20% activity, i.e., very important for your career, job, business or anything important, you must be focusing and delivering that activity.

Moreover, this 80:20 Principle has already pruned out a larger number of your activities (either to be done later or to be spent minimal time thereupon), so this should be greater motivation for your mind to not to procrastinate such activity.

12: Develop Keystone Habit-Enjoy Ripple Effect

A keystone habit (also called a cornerstone habit) is a habit which brings up a chain of other good habits, following and as a result of the cornerstone habit. Let's understand this by way of a simple example.

Suppose you work on developing the habit of a daily walk in the early morning. Once you start cementing this daily habit of a morning walk, it will prompt you on its own to develop a chain of certain other habits, like:

- You will start waking up early morning.
- While walking you may easily club another habit of listening to great audiobooks or podcast alongside. (Walking and listening will take care of your physical health and mental health, respectively)
- You will not binge-watch TV late nights and sleep earlier at night.
- Once you start getting the good feeling of a vibrant and energetic health during your days, you will give up eating any unhealthy or junk food, which brings drowsiness or lazy feelings.
- To continue to feel better during your days, you will start eating healthier food.
- You will develop the habit of staying happy during the days.

You can see that by developing one keystone habit, you have developed multiple good habits alongside. This strategy can very well be applied to beat procrastination and start a chain reaction of manifold good habits.

Taking the above example of a single cornerstone habit of walking in the early morning, you would feel tons of physical and mental energy. There are good chances that your reasons for procrastination are feeling the lack of energy or vibrancy in your body, which will get cured by merely starting a one cornerstone habit.

Now let's take an example related to your work or workplace. Assuming you start developing a habit every evening after you are done with your work, of writing the 3-4 key activities, which you must have to do the next day in order to move forward to the next level of the project.

Once you develop that habit, it will have multiple benefits associated with it, which will help you effectively kill procrastination.

You will start seeing following positive effects every day for you, like below:

- You will have no stress on the next day after waking up, as you already know those key items that day lying on your desk needing your attention. You can quickly start working the very first thing in the morning on that activity (except in some cases, when some new priority has come up suddenly).
- Since you have a clearly focused list of activities, you will be vigilant enough not to waste your time gossiping or chit-chatting on trivial subjects with your other colleagues or co-workers.
- Since you have to focus on 3-4 key tasks only during the day instead of seeing in the form of a mega project, it doesn't feel overwhelming to you. So, you have already started eating the elephant one bit at a time. This way you can avoid the tendency to procrastinate, which generally arises in the wake of the feeling of overwhelming.

So, you would notice very quickly, as to how working on developing the keystone habits can work wonders to beat the procrastination monster and help you reach the level of peak performance.

Now you should do some brainstorming and choose a keystone habit for you to start a chain reaction of other good habits.

13: Busy Life is Easy Life

As they say: ***"Busy Life is an easy Life"***

At times, it will happen that you feel like you not moving anywhere. It might seem like a very long tunnel with no light appearing to come sooner to you. In such situation, you may feel demoralized to take any further action on the project. You start to think that despite so many hard efforts, things are not moving in the way, you had planned. You are on the verge of quitting or giving up. You will strongly feel the instinct to procrastinate taking actions on your key priorities.

Before we address this, let's have a look at this good piece of advice. Seth Godin in his famous book titled **"The Dip: The extraordinary benefits of knowing when to quit (and when to stick),"** has precisely explained three types of situations namely, cliff, *cul-de-sacs* and Dip for helping you decide on quitting on anything.

He advised that only in the case of '*cul-de-sec*' (French word for "dead-end") situation, which is a phase when you are sure that despite hardest efforts, the project you are working on will not yield you that outcome, which you have been working hard for. So, in such a situation, it is good advice to quit. But in this case, where you had been working on your project, which you have chosen, because this project has the potential to lead you to your dream destination, then don't quit.

"Winners don't quit. Quitters don't win" ~ Vince Lombardi

So now coming back to the key question- how to continue and be in the game, despite the feeling of leading to nowhere? How to stay put in what you do, if you are feeling so much frustrated and totally unwilling to put any further efforts?

One strategy, which has worked for me in the past very well, is to keep myself busy.

Let me explain it a bit. Any project, which you are in, may have multiple elements to work up. When you come across the situation of frustration or disappointment in your life, you should work on the simplest tasks. I mean the tasks, which are simply of the nature of quickly ticking the box. The basic idea here is to just show up at work and start working on the easiest portions of the project.

There is a beautiful quote from Woody Allen:

"Eighty Percent of success is showing up."

I have seen in my cases that once you have started and are into the game, then your creative juices start flowing. And in no time, you again start catching up with the difficult things.

That's the way our minds work. In fact, these are all thought clouds which blur our vision at times and overshadow the bigger picture of our goals. Then it becomes a vicious circle of negative thoughts blurring the vision, and the blurred vision further demoralizes us to put any action towards that. When no action happens, so obviously no results will appear. So, our approach should be to break the chain of these thoughts as soon as possible. And the best way is not to allow the mind to think (these negative thoughts) and keep it busy in the productive parts. It doesn't matter how simple the task is. But just keep the mind on business. As you all know from ages:

"An idle mind is devil's workshop."

Stephen King, the world-famous fiction author (net worth of more than USD 400 Million), writes about his daily ritual as below:

He states that he does not wait for motivation to arrive at him to start working. He starts working daily at 8 a.m., regardless of how-so-ever he feels and eventually motivation has to come forward to keep him going. He has been following this daily practice of writing rigorously for so many years, and now he has reached a stage that he does not need any motivation to start working on the things. That's the power of showing up and staying in the game for long enough.

So, the takeaway for beating the procrastination habit is:

<u>Just show up at the activity and start doing it. If not difficult portions, start with the simpler aspects of the project. But the key point is just to start the activity and keep you busy.</u>

It can be compared to like "bringing the horse to the water" theory. If you have to let your horse drink the water and it is not willing to, then you have to simply bring your horse to the water. You have to tell your mind horse to just show up at the water pond, i.e., in front of the activity to be undertaken. You can apply this strategy to every activity, which your mind allures you to defer to a later date.

This activity could be opening up the powerpoint slide to start that heavy appearing presentation for your next client meeting. Or it could be initiating the filing of your tax return, hitting the gym or going out for a run.

But you have to show up and start doing it by choosing the simplest and easiest aspect of your project or activity.

14: Pre-commit to the World

There is another good way, but a really hard one to beat procrastination and jump start into action instantly.

Pre-commit to the activity publicly.
Once you have done your internal assessment of the project and the timelines it will take, then you make a declaration to your own world, small or big. Though you may not have access to print media or television about your commitment, in the modern high-tech digital world, there are so much faster social media tools to share with the outside world about what you are up to. Your social media giant friend 'Facebook' daily morning asks you to share about how is your day today and prompts you to share your thoughts with the world.

Assuming you are preparing for half-marathon three months away from now. While you have started the training and diet program etc., but you tend to procrastinate at times going out for a run on a daily basis. What you need to do is to announce to your small world what project you are up to and when you are going to complete the same. This will put you into a situation of social pressure. In such situation, when you start delaying in the project, you will remember your commitment to the entire world. And then, you will gear up and work faster on that project. It happens that way because, if we don't keep our promises, then we are at the risk of losing our credibility and respect in our network. We are scared that nobody out there will take your words seriously.

Once you announce to your world, then your mind will immediately foresee the picture of being ridiculed or made fun of, if you are not able to live up to your words. So, the pain of being socially ridiculed or laughed at will frighten your mind. And then the mind will instantly push the procrastination monster aside and will help you keep going further on your key priority item.

15: Assessment Tool - Examine Adverse Effects of Procrastination

Remember, our minds are wired in such a way that they work to enhance the pleasure or avoid the pains. You can check-out any of your decisions of your past, and you would conclude that all the choices you have made so far in life are either to enhance the pleasure or to avoid the pain (take a moment to think, it's a fact!).

Even if the activities, which may seem to be creating pain currently, you chose to do because you will have pleasure in achieving the results later in the long run.

You might have been through the experience personally or would have seen people around you doing workout in the gym rigorously. Do you think that carrying heavy weights or doing those loaded squats is very joyful? No, not always!
But still, you see the people spending hours in the gyms to do those workouts. The

obvious reason is that though the instant cost of that activity is the feeling of pain in your muscles, the reward which you foresee doing this activity is a fit and perfectly shaped body. You know that by putting hard efforts and enduring the pain in the short run, you will be able to enjoy the heightened levels of fitness and even may flaunt your perfectly trimmed body in front of your friends.

Therefore, in your day to day life, whenever there is a feeling of postponing or delaying some activities, you should simply do this exercise of ascertaining well in advance (A) the future positive outcomes of doing that activity currently or else (B) the harmful effects in future by not carrying out the activity now.

Take an example:

You have been assigned a very important project or a new client to work with on a massive project. Now you need to open your assessment tool.

If you don't work on this important project or delay it beyond the committed timelines, then what is the impact?

- You may lose out the opportunity for your next promotion.
- You may get scolded by your boss.
- Maybe you will be running the risk of being terminated due to non-performance.
- That the client may post a negative review of your services, which may put your credibility at risk.

On the other hand, make your calculation of what will happen, if you complete the project well within time or maybe before that.

See, what will happen now?

- You will be appreciated by the organization or may be rewarded.
- Your client may give you additional work to handle, as he is satisfied with your delivery standards etc.
- You will feel very positive and motivated towards the life.

Now after doing all the assessment of procrastinating on a given work and ascertaining the pros and cons of both the actions scenarios, i.e., <u>procrastinating it</u> vs. <u>doing it in time</u>, your mind will choose the appropriate action. Obviously, it will do such activities, which will enhance the pleasure and also it will avoid doing such activities, which will cause pain for it.

So, whenever the next time you are plagued with procrastination in carrying out your key goals, you should use this assessment tool and it will guide you on the right set of action steps to move forward.

16: Step One-Clarity Rule

"A journey of a thousand miles begins with a single step"~ Lao-tzu.

If you precisely figure out at least the first step towards any big major project, then there is a high probability that you will start the work immediately. It doesn't mean that you need not require a detailed analysis or planning for work ahead of you. Of course, you have to have a plan in place.

But, I am talking about a scenario, when the whole planning thing is taking forever, and you are delaying the start of the project. In such a scenario it is advisable to get the details worked out for the initial step and get started (while in the back-end your planning on the next steps of the project may carry on). The idea behind this is when you are clear about what step is required to do, there is very less probability of mind trying to delay it further if the work is really an important one.

So, if the very first step of a bigger project, which is an overwhelming project, is explained, then you are left with no further excuse to delay or postpone the action. Also, it has a ripple effect too. As you jump into the first step of the project and finish that successfully, it generates a momentum. It generates a sense of confidence that you figured out the details of the first step and then further executed, which made the next steps clearer. As someone rightly stated:

"Daily small victories lead to winning the big battle."

Further, once you are into the project, you get to know the ground realities. You get to know the people or stakeholders involved. You may get to know someone who has got some experience in the further steps of the project and is willing to support and guide you in the project. The idea is that things start getting familiar and seem to be less overwhelming, once you start getting into the things.

Once you start finishing the initial steps of the project diligently and effectively, you gain momentum. And if you stick to the game, congratulations, you have already beaten the procrastination monster for that project.

17: Divide and Conquer Rule

Divide and conquer- this was the rule I heard in my school days.
We were taught in the history classes that it was the strategy which British colonizers used to follow to maintain their control over India. Following this rule, if they found Indians somewhere, who were getting united for a common cause toward the independence of their country, the

British officers used to play tricks to cause a divide amongst different factions of the society.

By causing such dispute amongst the different sections, they were able to dominate the smaller, fragmented set of people easily and maintain their kingdom over the country. Until the whole nation woke up and stood united towards a common cause, the divide and conquer rule was the key mantra for Britishers to dominate our country for ages.

The above analogy can be used in the context of beating procrastination. In other words, you can beat the procrastination monster by applying the Divide and Conquer Rule. You tend to procrastinate if the project is big and seems overwhelming. You tend to lose control on where to start and which portion to start. So, the best strategy here is to divide a huge project into bite-sized mini-projects.

For example, if you have to arrange a cultural event in your residential society or an annual event or a birthday party of your kid or inauguration ceremony of your store.

Whatever the task may be, you might think that this is the "one big event" or "one big activity" only. But in effect, it is a project, involving so many mini-set of activities, which need to be carried out either simultaneously or sequentially.

So, practically, what do you do to address this project?

- You split the activities by naming each activity separately.
- If you have people around you to participate, you will assign the roles to each to take care of the work separately.
- Since you need to hire a lot of outside vendors for catering, decoration or music, lights, cameras, etc., you will divide the number of activities into a mini project for each activity.
- Now if you are planning to do the anchoring of the event yourself, this activity needs preparation and rehearsal, which activity you will assign to yourself.

Once you have identified the multiple activities required to be done in the big project, you have to assign the timelines then to complete each activity by you, by vendors and by other team members to complete the project. Here you can see, you have divided a big project into so many smaller activities, some to be done by your friends, some outside vendors, and some by you.

I know, while teaching by way of an example, this seems to be quite obvious and a no-brainer, but when we have to apply this practically as a strategy, it seems overwhelming. But let me tell you all the projects, whether it is setting up a new railway line or constructing a huge dam on the river or even sending the rocket to space, all require bite-sizing of the projects into mini-set of activities.

In fact, there is no other way. Without dissecting into a smaller portion, every task has a monstrous size and difficult to cope up with.

But, all this is a matter of practice and training your brain to take control of the things and focus on bite-sized mini-projects to be achieved in a given timelines.

18: Replace Negative Self-Talk with Positive Thoughts

We already discussed this in the previous chapter. all kind of reasons why we do procrastinate. All the reasons somehow have the element of negative self-talk. One way or the other, we keep on telling something negative about ourselves, about situations about other people. Take any type of reasons for procrastination; the element of negative talk comes into the picture in below ways:

- You think that work is too big for you to handle.
- You tell yourself that you don't have that skill or experience to handle that activity.
- You confuse yourself by saying that the circumstances are not in your favor to carry on that activity as of now.
- You falsely tell yourself that you don't have all the required resources to complete that activity

- And so on, the list keeps on going.

But it is my personal experience that all these talks generally are very far from the truth. I am not advocating building castles in the air, but blatantly blaming the circumstances or continuously doubting your capabilities is not a virtue. As we all know:

"Thoughts become things, choose them wisely"~ Mike Dooley

The suggestion here is to get yourself in contact with some inspirational stuff on a regular basis. This is required to counter the impact of the negative self-talk going on in your heads. Get to read something uplifting on a daily basis to boost your morale and confidence regularly. There is a logical reasoning behind this. And you can vouch for this from your practical experience so far in your life.

The kind of negative self- talks or blaming the outside environment is (a) generated or formed in our minds only and (b) only because of the environment we choose to be in.

I am emphasizing here that we choose to be in certain environments on our own. Some of you might be thinking now about questions like, *"I have to live with a particular type of relative due to my personal reasons, as I don't want to create a stress situation in my house."*

Yes, here we have some practical solutions to be positive even in the negative environments, if you think you have to spend time with such persons due to certain compulsions. Still, there is a solution. You can be with that person and still choose to be insulated from his or her negativity, rather using that time to build upon positivity or building skills.

But you will ask, how? A simple and practical strategy! You can listen to podcasts, which are free to download and then listen offline on your smartphone. One of the most recommended podcasts for people to deal with emotional issues is from my virtual mentor, Brooke Costillo, whom I followed a lot when I was going through the heights of negativity due to my surrounding uncontrollable environment. She is such a person that you would feel like she is addressing your direct issues. You can reach her at her podcast at https://thelifecoachschool.com/category/p odcasts/.

Also, you can listen to audiobooks available at www.audible.com. I believe they had a plan for starters to get first two audio books for free (get details at my website in recommended resources section).

It is all mind's BS, which you don't need to pay attention to, rather you have to replace this with the positive thoughts and create a positive environment around you. In my earlier book "Master Your Day- Design Your life," I have created one detailed chapter on **"How to deal smartly with the outside world,"** which addresses how to handle all such outside environment in a very smart way (with minor steps or tweaks).

With all the positive thoughts, you don't have the reasons to delay or postpone the work, due to the negativity created by yourself only.

19: Meditation – A Laser Beam to pierce Procrastination.

We all know that our minds are jumping around all the time like monkeys (probably, we haven't yet totally forgotten our long-ago ancestors). Thanks to this monkey mindset, most of us keep on jumping from one distraction to another and are not able to achieve significant results in different areas of our life.

As we all know, success requires a laser-sharp focus on one activity at a time and you need to persistent on that path. But distractions are the biggest hurdles in the way. Distractions are everywhere, at work and at home too. You get distracted at the office, and you get distracted at the movie theatre too. The conclusion is that we are not where we are physically present. We are not into the very activity we are doing at any point in time. If we are in the office, we think of home. If we are watching some good movie, thoughts come up about the office and we start checking our emails there. So, we rarely are in the present moment.

The cure to procrastination is to be in the present moment. Do the activity which matters most and be present totally. If we can implement that cure, the procrastination monster is nipped in the bud. But how do we come to the present moment?

The answer is silence or meditation.

Our minds are like a glass of water filled with dust particles. So, the default nature of our mind is clean and pure water. Our thoughts are like mud and make the water shady or dusty. Therefore, the solution to this is to allow the glass to be put straight for a few minutes and not allow any movement in the water. You will see that mud and water get separated in some time.

Similarly, meditation or staying in silence for just 10 minutes a day (on a regular basis) allows you to reach that stage, where all your thoughts get settled below, and you start receiving clearer messages from the universe, which are beneficial or helpful to you. Distraction is the biggest attractor for procrastination. You procrastinate easily if any distraction allures you for a quick dose of entertainment.

The idea of meditation or silence is to build the focus muscle. If you can sit idle doing nothing for a 10-minute period, that means you have been able to repel all the distraction during that time.

In fact, meditation has dual benefits. One, it allows you to see your monkey thoughts jumping from here and there from a distant place. You get disengaged from your mind for some time to understand its real game. Another benefit is that you practice coping with the distractions coming at the time of meditation as well. With practice, you can be able to repel any kind of distractions, which may arise during your work time as well.

Therefore, with the help of daily meditation for just 10 minutes a day, you will start learning to watch the distractions. And very soon, you will realize that you are enhancing your focus significantly on the work, which on its own beats the procrastination beast.

20: Drastically Limit Alternatives

One of the main reasons we procrastinate is that we give ourselves many options to choose from. We put a lot of stuff on the table and then simply expect the mind to focus on the one most important thing. Take an example.

If you keep a very informative and inspiration autobiography book in front of you and alongside that you keep multiple other online games or magazines or excitingly looking junk foods, what will be your instant reaction? For most of the people, the chances are that they will be required to spend a lot of mental energy to pick up the resourceful book when they are given so many distractive choices.

Alternatively, if before a reasonable person (like you and me – because I love writing this literature and you are reading this ☺), only very limited number of options are presented, then we would directly get into the most productive activities.

You see, even the productive and reasonably disciplined people get into the trap of distraction if given numerous choices. You remember the instant gratification theory I explained in the initial chapters of this book. On the one hand, we are convinced that the book is going to help us in the longer term to improve our lives and make our performance better by learning the strategies followed by great people. On the other hand, we are clear that other alternatives given to us are giving us the instant gratification, i.e., a short-term instant reward. So, the mind has to put its energy into comparing the immediate reward v/. future reward.

So, my submission is that, wherever things are in our control, we should not waste our minds' energy and our willpower in making simple choices like this. Why do we, in the first place, give such alternatives to our mind, which we know clearly that these are not going to serve our purposes?

For example:

- Why keep lots of ice-creams and chocolates or other junk foods in our refrigerators when we can store nutritious fresh fruits and vegetable there?

- Why do we present our minds with attention stealing online games or entertainment magazines etc., when we can fill our showcases with resourceful books?
- Also, why do we stuff up our houses with indoor games and mess up our health, when we can grab the outdoor sports equipment to motivate our minds to get out of our houses, which will bring us in nature and also make us somewhat social too.

So, if you want to avoid procrastination on the important activities, don't let the concentration of your mind bog down with multiple unproductive choices. Keep your desk and workplaces very clean and devoid of any kind of distractions. This way, your mind will have least possible options to procrastinate; rather it can directly allow you to jump into the most productive activity.

I was reading somewhere that Apple founder Steve Jobs was asked once why he always keeps his office and entire decorum as totally white and clean without any paintings or other decorative materials, etc. His answer was simple, *"I want to see everything totally clean in front of me. White is the symbol of total clarity and deprived of any kind of distractions. This allows me and my team to focus clearly on the work and breeds in innovative ideas to build better product features"*.

So, you see, a legend has been formed by not giving any distracting options to the mind. Limit the distractions to zero or minimize to the best possible extent and you will be able to kill the procrastination monster with least efforts.

21: Be Comfortable with Discomfort

Yes, undoubtedly, this is the game changer. It requires a mindset shift, but this shift is worth it. Because the kind of reward, you will be giving yourself is tremendous. If you love your discomfort, what will you do next?

Of course, you will be choosing all your discomforts and move towards them and take action to make them comfortable for you. One of the biggest advantages of this strategy is that you will always be in your comfort zone.

Oh, this seems strange, but how?

Because your comfort zone gets enhanced every time, you choose to work on your discomforts. One of the prime reasons for procrastination is that you think that the work before you will put you in an uncomfortable position. So, the natural tendency would be to avoid doing that work.

Assuming you have been assigned work by your boss, if you are in a job or if you are on your own, your customer or client wants you to get some work done with a tight timeline. Unfortunately, and sadly, that works requires you to engage with a co-worker or any other third party, which you don't like or it doesn't appeal to you. But, if you choose this discomfort and apply this "love your discomfort" strategy, what will you expect to happen?

The straightforward benefit is that you will get your work done and make your boss or client happy and satisfied. Your other colleagues or competitors might have chosen not to work on this for similar reasons as you first thought, but you chose to love your discomfort and executed the work. So, the immediate reward is the mental satisfaction of getting the work done along with the additional perks of improved credibility and the possible financial rewards.

Secondly, you will give yourself a chance to explore another persons' perspective too. Maybe you might come to know that the person was a nice fellow to work with, but his outside facade or outer world interaction was representing somehow otherwise. You improve your social skills very much by this methodology.

I remember an instance in my college days. I think myself as an introverted person, who loves to be with myself and has a very limited closed circle of people, I can relate to. So, this was the case, in the initial days, when I moved to college. A few days later, I became friends with 2-3 people, and I mean good friends. One fine day, I got a sudden spark of revelation, when my friend told me his very first opinion about me.

I was surprised to know that he initially thought me as an arrogant and self-centered person (no, introvert does not mean that at all, we simply enjoy ourselves a lot) and who doesn't like other persons. He further clarified that it was his first impression, but after engaging with me, he found me a genuine person to be with.

This personal example was to put across the point that we might have all the stories in our heads about other people, which sometimes, might be far away from the truth.

We live in our mind-generated realities only. We view our world only as per our perception of the people around or our circumstances. The same things may be viewed very differently by another person, based on his own thought-generated realities. I think we digressed a bit, but it was required to convey the message thoroughly.

So, this was one kind of discomfort we encounter. There could be X number of discomforts, which one may have. The idea is to keep looking at your discomfort and keep taking action on them.

Again, as told, this would require a total mindset shift and not an easy one. But, the efforts in this direction are worth putting out because the rewards are immense with the possibility of exponential growth in a very short period. This will cure your procrastination problem forever, and moreover, it will present you endless opportunities for personal and professional growth.

22: Insulate yourself from Digital Distractions

Digital Distractions!

This is another demon and today's biggest contributor and feeder to the procrastination beast. It drastically slows down our progress towards any specific goal. Whatever important activity you are into, that one notification sound on your Smartphone, maybe an email notification, WhatsApp message or Facebook notification or twitter beep, has a superpower to get the status of the most important activity in that very moment.

The instant curiosity of that one moment makes you so restless to check that notification instantly as if every such message will be requiring instant attention or top priority. You can't stop your craving to look at your smartphone. You might be wondering it might be some important email from your client or your boss, which needs urgent attention.

Yes, your worry is genuine sometimes. After all, human beings have developed all this technology to be super-efficient by increasing the flow of information so that urgent activities can be addressed quickly.

But here is the catch. Except for very few matters, all digital notifications cannot be appearing with a badge of *"I am Most important"* in front of you. Here, the objective is to minimize the digital distraction to the best possible extent. You need to build on some standard operating procedures (SOP) and bring in the discipline in implementing that SOP.

So how should we address this?

Here is the approach which I follow personally and suggest to you. At the start of your day, you must have already earmarked the important activities and assigned the priorities regarding committed deliverables.

Now, you have to divide the digital distractions into two categories:

- Work-related notifications
- General news/social media updates.

We will handle both types of distractions separately. Let's take up the important one first, i.e., work-related notifications and do the following.

For email notification, assign a specific rule, for emails coming from a specific set of persons, who are important, i.e., your boss or your 1-2 subordinates (working closely with you on any project) or your top 3 clients (giving maximum revenues).

Now pay attention. The rule is to make the notification bar off or notification tone in silent mode for a specific number of hours in a day, when you want to address your important project activities. The only exception is your identified list of people, for which you will assign a specific notification tone.

This is the exception, because, you know very well, these people may change your priorities instantly. After all, you are doing all your tasks for your superior in the office or your client, and if he or she wants a different priority, then you have to adhere to it.

Similarly, nowadays WhatsApp is being used as an effective tool in most of the office communication. Here, also make all the notifications silent except specific individuals or work-related projects groups, where your immediate inputs may be required. This will drastically reduce your digital distraction. If you were getting a *hundred* beeps in an hour, then by this way, you may be getting *ten* such beeps.

Sounds a little bit relaxing, right?

So, you can keep yourself focused on work, and your mind won't have any excuse to procrastinate your key activities. Then assign a specific number of times a day, maybe 3-4 times a day, when you would spend 15 minutes or so in reviewing all other messages. This will help you to reprioritize the activities, if something else may need to be handled urgently. Trust me, this will work for you. It worked for me to focus my attention on work.

Now let's address the second category of distraction- General News/Social Media Updates

Nothing much to say here! A simple rule to follow! Rather, I would say the simplest one. Just put the notification tones and pop-ups disabled and review your all notification after your working hours. Only for 15-30 minutes a day. This is just to keep you updated on the stuff going on.

Some of you may think that you won't, on your own, be able to control your cravings. Then, you may need some 'guardian' for controlling your cravings. Fortunately, you can *'adopt'* few guardians, thanks to the technology to help you out by restricting your access to these social media monsters stealing your attention. Though, it would sound like putting passwords on certain apps, before giving your phone to your kid :). But let's admit, some of us (still kids from inside) really need that to whack our procrastination habits.

I just approached "Dr. Google" once to prescribe me some good apps to restrict the access to social media giants. Surprising, the number of results were more than a million. I only tested a few apps little bit and found them to be useful to avoid digital distractions. Here are these:

Stay focused: you can dedicate the amount of time per day, allowed for watching the social media sites, as you may list in the app. Remember your strict hostel warden with a stick to control your TV watching time in the earlier days.☺.

Another one is "**Cold turkey**", which has the similar objective, i.e., to block certain sites for specified numbers.

For those, who after self-reflection, realize that social media or digital distraction is the biggest factor causing them to procrastinate, are a tool worth exploring. Of course, there are tons of others, and one can fill a large volume of the book with such tactics, but that is not the sole topic of this book, so we need to move on to the next strategy now.

But, if you find some other tool, which you feel great after implementing, you may want to put your comment on my site @ www.sombathla.com or my Facebook Page at https://www.facebook.com/sombathla1. I have a habit of reviewing comment from my readers.

23: 4D/A Rule

The 4D/A rule is on the premise that for any activity in front of you, you have to make either of these choices amongst 4Ds and A. Next time any activity, which comes to you, you have to test that activity on the barometer of 4D/A. It means you have to categorize that activity into any of the below-stated actions:

- **D**elete it;
- **D**efer it,
- **D**elegate;
- **D**o it,
- **A**utomate it.

If you follow the above practices of categorizing your work activities amongst the above parameters that would never make you feel overwhelmed. The reason behind that is for the first three kinds of decisions, it is not coming to your "immediate" basket, so you make your 'current' action list uncluttered.

Generally speaking, there could be an only limited number of activities that would require your immediate attention. Also, if you see the last two categories, even in the case of activities, which you are supposed to handle yourselves, you have two choices. Either you can do it yourself, or you may consider automating the process by putting some additional time in building some system or processes, so that next time, it gets done on an automated basis.

Just to elaborate it a little bit more: All the activities on your desk will need to go to either of the categories.

- **D**elete it - All the work coming to your desk needn't be done. Some emails or messages may be simply ignored, as they don't fit into your priority work list at all. Examples could be tons of email just marked a cc to you, which require no inputs from you and even no action from you in near future. Delete it here means delete from your to-do-activity list only. You may choose to retain those in your inbox for any future reference.

- **D**efer it - Defer it to a later time depending upon the level of prioritization.

- **D**elegate it - if you think, the work doesn't require specialized expertise of your level and another person can do it, delegate the work immediately.

- **D**o it. If the work does not fit into any of the above categories and it requires your specific involvement and use of your intellect (unless you can automate it further), then you have to plan to do it yourself in the committed timelines.

- **A**utomate it: If by using some systems and putting some time upfront, you can automate the work activity, which gets done on its own through the system, it's better to be done that way. One mini-example of automation could be setting up automated bill payments for your electricity, telephone, mobile, broadband, satellite TV, any magazine subscriptions, etc. It may take time once to set up those, but then, you never have to do it again for months and years.

Finally, if you keep thinking for a long time about assigning either of the "Ds" or A to any specific work, then, there is a caution sign that by your own indecision, you are even procrastinating in implementing this procrastination beating technique. This is a strange situation (and unfortunately, there is no quick fix solution, you have to discipline your mind here)!

So next time, whenever you are taking stock of the items earmark either of the four "D" or "A" on the item, make it a habit of doing it quicker, as this is going to be your tool to avoid any feeling of overwhelming due to work overload.

Thus, by minimizing the number of activities on your plate, you have a sense of liberation, and you can push the procrastination beast away from you.

24: Follow "Just in Time" Approach vs. "Just in Case" Approach

Tim Ferris, the best-selling author of "**4-Hour Work Week,**" has elaborated this principle. He states that our approach towards learning should be on "just in time" basis and not "Just in Case".

Let me explain it further and how it is relevant to beat the procrastination beast.

"**Just in case**" psychology prompts to consume every piece of information around us, on the premise that we may need it anytime in the near or distant future. It is a general norm, and the society around us teaches to consume everything as it might be helpful in some manner anytime.

This philosophy is only helpful to the extent of your boasting to the world about your knowledge. All the information gathered under this thought process is not immediately required or in most cases not required at all. Moreover, at the time, when it is needed, you would have already forgotten about the stuff and would be required to re-learn that stuff anyway.

But "**just in time**" psychology works on the premise that we should put our best efforts into learning something new only at a time when we need to complete our tasks.

In case, you are misinterpreting this, let me clarify here. I am not advocating or suggesting to reduce your information intake or knowledge updating. I am only suggesting to intake only that information, which is immediately needed to help your current work going on.

Let me try to put it by way of an example.

I worked as a lawyer in a substantial part of my career so far. So, one needs to be totally updated about the legal developments happening around to provide the expert solution to your employer or your client basis the latest legal position. But here is how we need to apply the "Just in Time" principle. If I am working in an FMCG (fast moving consumer goods) company, every amendment in the laws related to FMCG Industry is "just in time' information, because any update may require you to change your business strategy.

But beware, any information related to telecom laws or media laws is only a 'just in case' information. You will not need it now, but, in future, if you happen to join some telecom or media company or any law firm, you may need to have an update on all the laws, in which you practice.

You may find tons of other examples in your day to day affairs, when "Just in Case" syndrome has distracted you from your main priorities.

But, how does this help to address procrastination?

'Just in case' principle prompts you to consume the information, which is not required as of now. For that matter "just in case' information is a distraction and will pull you away from your key priorities, on the premise that you might need it in the future. You will get one more excuse to procrastinate your key activity.

To put it simply, "Just in time" would significantly reduce the chances of your procrastinating the work currently on your plate. Because, you are not getting bugged by 'just in case' bug and consuming everything, which ultimately distracts you. Rather you are working on your most important priorities, and if you need some information on that, immediately do your research on the limited point and get back to your work.

Remember, we stated already to reduce the number of distractions to the minimum. The side benefit of just in time consumption is that your level of understanding gets significantly enhanced because you are implementing the information simultaneously while you are learning it.

25: Batching – An Antidote to Procrastination

Batching principle is a big-time saver and an antidote to procrastination.

Batching simply means to put all the activities, which are of similar nature in one basket and then allocating a specific schedule to address that basket only. Take an example of your emails. There could be two ways of looking at your emails.

- One is on a real-time basis- i.e., the moment it comes, you want to see it and address it immediately.

- The other approach is to allocate a specific number of times, i.e., three times a day when you would see all the emails and address it.

I believe you got the point already. Looking at the emails on the real-time basis does not make you more productive, rather this will be a distraction to your already ongoing key priorities.

Supposing you are in a meeting with a client and listening to his/her requirement or you are working on some important article to be published soon, or it might be that you are working on a time-sensitive report to be sent to senior management in next few hours. If you are checking every email on real-time basis, there are good chances that you will be delaying the completion of your priority item, or you may produce a lower quality deliverable, which will be disrupting your credential before and may affect your work.

So, this was about batching your activity of addressing the emails.

In practical life, you do the batching of your routine already. Most of the people prefer to do the grocery buying once in a month (not on a daily basis). Also, instead of daily going to the supermart, you would prefer to buy your stocks of fruits and vegetable on a weekly basis. Even in the kitchen, you would be doing your dishes in 1-2 batches only, not now and then. This all is batching the activity in one slot instead of doing it in a scattered manner.

I don't know your work environment. I am not aware if you do a job, or a consultant or a freelancer, or a homemaker. But whosoever you are and whatsoever you do, the principles remain the same. Any scattered work activity doesn't motivate you; rather it distracts your attention, which in turn costs your other high rewarding activity. Therefore, you can have a look at your other schedule of activities, which could be batched to be done in one go.

In fact, batching of activities is the biggest motivator to kill procrastination. Batching allows you to perceive the activities differently. Firstly, you undertake to do all the similar activities in one go so that you can do everything in a flow state. It will save a lot of time for sure. Secondly, you are motivated because you know that you will be thrashing out multiple numbers of activities in one go.

Therefore, the batching of activities will convey a bigger picture to your mind of a substantial achievement, so there is a high probability that you won't be procrastinating on the activities already batched.

26: Use Checklists to Keep You under Check

This strategy works very well for activities, which are more of process oriented. That means, there is a sequence of activities to be done or certain things to be done in parallel.

We tend to procrastinate or get distracted by other things if every time we have to think of the next steps to be taken in the project. Generally speaking and in my personal experience as well, I have noted that certain activities are a combination of various mini-steps to be taken in that process.

I believe you might have a similar observation about certain types of activities. Let me again take an example from the legal domain.

While drafting or reviewing some agreement, which is a lengthy process and a substantial number of clauses are standard provisions to be covered in that agreement. So, what effective lawyers do is to formulate a checklist or standard operating process for drafting and reviewing the agreements. The checklist is tick the box document, and you simply keep moving in the process and keep ticking the items covered or addressed.

By this process, there is the least possibility of getting distracted by other things, because you know that there are standard 15-20 items (may vary in your case) to be ticked to complete the agreement. I don't know, in which field or domain you are in, but there are good chances that for most of the activities, you can sit down and develop some checklist.

Besides curbing your procrastination habit, it will give you various side benefits as well. Firstly, by over and over practice, this checklist will become part of your brain neuro pathways, and you will become instantaneous in your job. While others may struggle to do the activity, you may find this an effortless job. So, there would not be any reason for you to procrastinate such activities.

Secondly, once you make certain things standardized, it takes less and less time and gives you room to focus on other big activities in your career, health, relationship, adventure and other important areas of your life.

Try it out with simple process activity and then you can extend the scoping of this to any of your process based activities.

27: Design Your Own Environment (Yes you can!)

You might have already heard this famous quote from Jim Rohn:

"You are the average of the five people you spend the most time with."

The above quote is the crux of this point. Try to assess your circumstances, where you work presently. If you are continuously and very frequently putting off certain actions, despite knowing that this is going to hamper your progress on your way to faster success, then there must be something wrong with your working environment.

Sit down and think!

- Are you surrounded by people, who love gossiping or watching T.V or Netflix or cat videos in the name of entertainment to kill their time?
- Are your desk and surrounding stuff messed up, prompting you to not stand a moment more at your workplace?
- Are you unaware and thus not using the best productivity tools or technology to better address your work requirements?

If the answer to any of questions is yes, then you need to give a serious look at your environment. You have to work on building a great working environment around you to deliver the best quality of deliverables. Now, you would say that you can't always have control over your environment.

I would say, except for few exceptions, you can create or even <u>design your environment</u>.

How?

As I am a big fan of categorization, so let's make two categories here as well. Your surrounding environment can fall into two categories:

- Controllable
- Non-controllable

Let's talk about non-controllable environment first. Bear in mind that certain things, we can't change (or some cases, we are very much scared to change rather). If you are in a full-time job, but not very happy with your boss or your co-workers or say with your work profile or for any XYZ reason whatsoever, unless you are totally frustrated with the environment, you will not consider changing your job. So, in this case, this environment is your non-controllable environment.

Similarly, if you are staying with a partner or life partner and have decided to stay with him or her (despite some concerns) for bigger reasons (maybe for your kids or your family), you have chosen this to be your environment, which is again a non-controllable environment.

Acknowledging that we don't have control, gives us a sense of awareness. Because, now we have declared that we can't change our environment, so we can take next step, i.e., choose not to react or feel bad about this environment. Because only once you are conscious and have a complete awareness, then only you are prepared to take a leap in your life.

Awareness is like the sun. When it shines on things, they are transformed" ~ Thich Nhat Hanh

Okay, now let's forget what we can't change and focus on what we can change, i.e., things which are controllable. So even in the non-controllable environments, we can create controllable things. Let's talk through some examples:

- If you don't want to speak to your co-worker, put an earphone in your ears and pretend that you are on a call or listening to something related to work. Boom, you got a small taste of victory.
- Make your workplace or desk, so clean and well-arranged that it inspires you to sit and work longer there.
- Get yourself associated more with people who are performers and get involved in any work, which gives you the opportunity to work with such people.
- If you are not happy with the approach of your boss but like the work and the office environment. Then try to adapt yourself, as per boss's requirements and prioritize your work according to his

requirement. Offer him solutions to his problems.

If you try to look and analyze your circumstances, you will realize that there is much room for making changes or designing your environment, if you keep aside your negative emotions regarding few non-controllable situations.

You would notice that earlier, the same "you" who used to procrastinate taking action on important deliverables by blaming the non-controllable environment, now start building own "controllable environment," in which there is a far more possibility of beating procrastination and being super productive by own choice.

CHAPTER 7: 7 DAYS PROCRASTINATION BEATING CHALLENGE

****

"Challenges are what make life interesting. Overcoming them is what makes them meaningful" ~ *Anonymous*

As you know, our minds like novelty and want some challenge to add some spice to the life. That's the reason we crave for moving out of our house every weekend to try new food, new restaurants, new movies in the town, etc. For the similar reasons, we want to have a big travel plan once or twice in a year, to give our minds a different experience.

Similarly, to beat our procrastination habits, we can make some fun and give our minds some new experience out of it. The other day, I was listening to Robin Sharma, the best-selling author of multiple personal development books (including "The Monk who sold his Ferrari") and I find his suggestion quite intriguing and worth exploring. He suggested that for 30 days consistently, choose one particular type of procrastination habit every day and try to make a victory over that habit. You don't need to go big. You just need to set some example in your mind to give it a different perspective on how does it feel when you win over procrastination.

I suggest starting even much smaller. Start with a seven days procrastination challenge, which is a reasonable period, short enough to get your mind convinced to at least try it and long enough to see if you can stick to this practice and then replicate the same further to another set of your procrastination habits.

So, you can list out of a lot of activities, which you generally procrastinate or which don't excite you, but you have to do it. I know you might try to procrastinate to try this free challenge. I am suggesting some hints for you to get started.

- Making your bed today.

- Get your clothes and accessories for tomorrow ready for the night before.
- Putting on the sports shoes ready in the night before and just move out of the house, for the sake of your fitness.
- Making that phone call to your friend, which you have been deferring for weeks.
- Mow your lawn.
- Spending 30 minutes with your kids (if you don't have kids, find something else exciting to spend time with)

Try to win over these seemingly small activities, just to give your mind a habit of winning and later we can even put big mountains in front of it to move, and I mean it. Because.

"If world problems feel too big to tackle, think small. Step by Step. Small wins build confidence, lead the way to change" ~ Rosabeth Moss Kanter

Thank You!

Before you go, I would like to say thank you for purchasing and reading my book.

You could have picked amongst dozens of other books on this subject, but you took a chance and checked out this one.

So, big thanks for downloading this book and reading all the way to the end.

Now I'd like to ask for a small favor. **<u>Could you please spend a minute or two and leave a review for this book on Amazon?</u>**

This feedback will help me continue to write the kind of Kindle books that help you get results.

And if you loved it, please let us know.

Your Free Gift Bundle:

Did you download your Gift Bundle already?

Click and Download your Free Gift Bundle Below

You can also download your gift at http://sombathla.com/freegiftbundle

Claim Your Gift Bundle!

Three AMAZING BOOKS for FREE on:

1. Mind Hacking - in just 21 days!
2. Time Hacking- How to Cheat Time!
3. The Productivity Manifesto

Download Now

instruction or commands. The reader is responsible for his or her own actions.

Adherence to all applicable laws and regulations, including international, federal, state, and local governing professional licensing, business practices, advertising, and all other aspects of doing business in any jurisdiction in the world is the sole responsibility of the purchaser or reader.